Northe...
The La...
Milan

from Lake Maggiore to Lake Idro

Jarrold Publishing

CONTENTS

Introducing the Italian lakes
Essential details in brief	3
Mountains and lakes	8
Life in Lombardy	11
Music and festivals	12
Signposts of history	14
Phases of history	15
For the art-lover	18
Food and drink	20
Shopping	25

Hints for your holiday	26
Where to go and what to see	27
Lake Maggiore	27
Lake Como	44
Lake Lugano	56
Milan	61
Historic towns in the shadow of the Alps	76
Lake Iseo	83

Useful things to know	89
Before you go	89
Getting to the Italian lakes	89
During your stay	90
Useful words and phrases	94
Index	95

Maps and plans
Lake Maggiore and Lake Orta	28
Lake Como	45
Lake Lugano	57
Milan	68–69
Brescia	77
Cremona	79
Lake Iseo	84
Lake Idro	88
General map	back cover

Title page: Isola Bella from Pallanza, Lake Maggiore

Isola di San Giulio, Lake Orta

Introducing the Italian lakes

Glorious lakeside days in northern Italy. And all because of thousands of years of unremitting Ice Age toil by giant hands long since melted away. Here where once the icy fingers of great alpine glaciers scoured out valleys large and small, you can enjoy all manner of holidays, from the most exclusive to the most affordable, amid subtropical vegetation on lakeland shores.

Lakes with poetry in their names draw the northern visitor across the Alps, but also cast their spell over the fortunate Italians from Turin and Milan. The largest lakes are Como, Maggiore and Lugano, the last of which extends to the very foot of the massive snow-capped mountains of Switzerland. But the sleepy Varesotto lakes, the tiny Lago di Mergozzo and the mysterious Lake Orta are certainly none the worse for being smaller. Lakes Iseo and Idro are now establishing themselves in the holiday world, slowly emerging from the shadow of Lake Garda, their illustrious neighbour.

For all their variety these lakes have something in common which cannot fail to appeal. They are protected by the mighty chain of mountains at their backs from the discomforts of often biting northerly and easterly winds. Despite all their scenic differences they bear the impress of a common culture, the culture of Lombardy. True, they extend beyond the boundaries of present-day Lombardy into the Tessin and Piedmont, but even so the unity of language, dialect, art and architecture is not to be denied.

Here is a land where lemons thrive, and where the mild climate encourages a multitude of subtropical plants into riotous bloom. Sometimes hidden amongst them, sometimes visible from afar, the shining white villas and *palazzi* of ancient noble families sit enthroned above the lakesides, a feast for the eye inside as well as out with their collections of Italian old masters. Here also are luxuriously ornate Baroque churches and nobly elegant Romanesque cathedrals. And all in addition to the lakes themselves, with their wealth of opportunities for sports of every kind.

Away from the colourful lakefront promenades with their cheerful, pulsating crowds is a tranquil hinterland abounding in contrasts. Mantua's art treasures wait to be discovered; secluded artists' colonies, at Bergamo perhaps, wait to be explored; traces of dim prehistory wait to be examined among the rock drawings of the Camonica Valley. In the mountains, on a ramble through narrow steep-sided valleys, you find eerie 'dying' villages off the beaten track, where a few elderly hill farmers live their timeless lives and the young people have long since migrated to the industrial cities or the tourist centres on the lakes. In the course of such walks unforgettable views constantly unfold and climbs are rewarded with unexpected glimpses of glittering lakes, bathed in sunshine of Mediterranean intensity.

For some connoisseurs of travel the time to visit Lombardy is in autumn – for the grape harvest with its convivial village festivals in the Valtellina and the Oltrepò Pavese. For others it is in winter because there is no better skiing to be found than in Bormio, Livigno or Madesimo. And how many opera- and music-lovers come for just a weekend, to hear great singing at La Scala in Milan?

Milan – the unacknowledged capital

La Scala! What better excuse to talk about Milan, 'mistress of Lombardy', much admired and much slandered, as are all who enjoy success. Milan is certainly one of the world's great cities, its population of 1.5 million swelling to almost 3 million when the inhabitants of its environs are included. It is a city whose name is synonymous with success, the brain and the brawn of the Italian economy – host to international fairs, centre of fashion, media colossus and chief among markets. The world's finest

La Scala Opera House, Milan

Dome of the Galleria Vittorio Emanuele, Milan

masters of modern design work here; Italy's major publishers and largest private television companies are located here; the country's biggest circulation daily newspaper *Corriere della Sera* is published here. Milan's is a way of life all its own – cultivating luxury without asking the price. The economic success of Italy's unacknowledged capital is plain enough for all to see but there is so much more to the city that no brief excursion could ever do justice to it. There is, for instance, the cathedral, and next to it the Galleria Vittorio Emanuele, the glass shopping-arcade unrivalled by any in the world. And there is Leonardo da Vinci's *Last Supper*. Despite extraordinarily expensive attempts at restoration nobody yet knows whether it can be saved.

In love with this bounteous and beautiful place . . .

At weekends the people of Milan like to make the one-hour drive to Lake Maggiore or Lake Como. These are (after Lake Garda) the largest of northern Italy's lakes, their combined surface area an impressive 358 sq km. Even in the last century the French writer Stendhal waxed lyrical about them: 'What is there to say about Lake Maggiore and Lake Como: one can only feel pity for anyone not in love with them.'

Konrad Adenauer, first Chancellor of West Germany, was certainly in love with this bounteous and beautiful place, and Cadenabbia, the fashionable retreat on the west bank of Lake Como, became even more famous because of him. In the 1950s the Villa La Collina high above the lake was his refuge from the exhausting burden of government in Bonn.

Introducing the Italian lakes

Cadenabbia, Locarno, Como, Stresa, Griante, Bellagio, Tremezzo are names with a ring to them, radiating a nostalgia for the *fin de siècle*. At the beginning of this century they were the exclusive playground of European high society. Even the outbreak of war in 1914 could not totally disrupt life in these summer resorts where Europe's aristocracy still gathered and gambolled while the world collapsed around them in rubble and ashes. The circle of privilege was only widened in the golden twenties, when kings were joined by composers, politicians and industrialists, by 'upstarts' and 'outsiders'. It was as if these newcomers felt themselves liberated by the beauty of the place, by the gentle climate and the scope for extravagance and eccentricity.

Behind the thick cypress hedges enclosing spacious gardens and the white walls of expensive villas many a folly was committed, with many a lapse from morality and good taste. At Ascona on Lake Maggiore one Berlin doctor, a disciple of Freud, acquired a highly dubious reputation for holding sex and cocaine orgies. Another German, a millionaire called Steindamm, caused a similar stir with nocturnal seances intended to provide proof of his claim to be Mozart reincarnated!

Nowadays life is quieter on the lakesides, and wealth is borne with more discretion. The people of the communities around the *laghi* have long since learnt that it is not the rich few but the average many – from not only Italy but also her neighbours – on whom prosperity depends today, and so they have responded accordingly. Hotels and pensions, and an increasing number of restaurants, now recognise that high standards of service are expected, but at reasonable prices.

For many holidaymakers a trip to the Italian lakes is complete with boats and *boccia*, a bathe and a stroll. There is, to be sure, little wrong with that, but it is looking at only one face of this lovely holiday area. Make the climb to a lonely mountain village, discover for yourself one of the many art treasures, take time to walk through magnificent gardens of cypresses and mimosa bushes, palms and magnolias, and a second face is suddenly revealed. Why not explore this most delightful of places with its two different faces – and many more besides?

Isola dei Pescatori, Lake Maggiore

Essential details in brief

Name: Repubblica Italiana (Republic of Italy). In ancient times northern Italy was called Insubria; today its name is Lombardia.

Founded: The republic was established on June 2nd 1946. The constitution came into force on January 1st 1948.

Form of government: Parliamentary democracy, headed by the state president who is elected for seven years. Parliament consists of two chambers, the *Camera dei Deputati* (Chamber of Deputies), with 630 members, and the *Senato della Repubblica* (Senate), with 315 senators elected by the regions. The maximum duration of a parliament is five years.

Administration: Italy is divided into regions, provinces and districts. Lombardy is one of twenty regions. The provinces of Lombardy are Bergamo, Brescia, Como, Cremona, Mantua, Milan, Pavia, Sondrio and Varese.

Language: Italian.

Religion: 97% Roman Catholic; Protestant (500,000), Jewish (35,000), other minorities.

Population: Italy: approx. 57 million. 8.9 million people live in Lombardy, about 16% of the total.

Pop. growth: 0.6% per annum.

Capital: Rome (pop. 3.5 million). Chief town of Lombardy: Milan (pop. 1.5 million).

Area: Italy: 301,278 sq km including Sardinia and Sicily. The Lombardy region covers 23,856 sq km, making it fourth largest in Italy, after Sicily, Piedmont and Sardinia.

Major exports: Machinery, motor cars, fashions, chemicals, pasta, cheese, vegetables, fruit, wine, oil, fish, rice.

Major imports: Iron, steel, wheat.

Villa Carlotta (above) and sailing at Lake Como

Mountains and lakes

Holiday companies and tour managers are in something of a dilemma when it comes to producing their glossy brochures on the Italian lakes. Who is it, after all, that they are trying to attract? Is it those holidaymakers with *dolce far niente* on their minds, in search of the ideal place to do no more than delightfully while away the time? Is it perhaps the sports enthusiast? Or is it rather the tourist with an interest in the culture and history of this richly endowed region? Those who do opt for two or even three weeks of the now popular combination of sun and water can certainly indulge themselves here on the shores of the Italian lakes. And who can blame them if they do? Don't we all want to relax first, to switch off and simply be lazy after the strains of a busy and burdensome year? But generally speaking this will not be enough for the kind of holidaymakers who come to the lakes. Action is what they tend to prefer, determined to make the most of the area's limitless opportunities. Those whose chief holiday ambition is to acquire the richest possible suntan will in fact usually bypass the *laghi*, feeling presumably that the beaches of the nearby Adriatic coast can offer them more. The lakeland holidaymaker on the other hand looks first to the water – there is certainly enough of it around! Over and above the twenty or so large and not so large lakes there are innumerable smaller and less frequented lakelets scattered throughout Lombardy. In all there is 1,000 sq km of water.

Superb sailing, and a pleasureland for motorboats

Sailing and motorboating are the two most popular watersports on the large expanses of Lakes Maggiore, Como and Lugano. Conditions are ideal, especially for sailing. On the northern parts of the lakes in particular the light breezes blowing down from the Alps almost always guarantee good progress through the water, and unexpected storms are few and far between. Members of British sailing clubs who have trailed their own boats over the Alps will find a welcome at the well-appointed marinas scattered around the lakes. More detailed information can be obtained from the Italian Sailing Association (*Federazione Italiana della Vela*, c/o Lega Navale, 19 Via San Vittore, 20123 Milan).

To the chagrin of some, but to the delight of many, no other lakeland area in Europe can lay claim to as many motorboats as this. Stately motor-yachts with white-painted deck saloons are definitely less in vogue than open-topped speedboats with powerful engines. Bow to bow, devouring fuel, these sporty craft roar from Como to Cadenabbia and from Luino to Angera, at the wheel a wealthy designer from Milan or a Frenchman who has made a million on the Stock Exchange. Both sailing boats and motorboats are available for hire for those who haven't brought their own. Enquire at local tourist offices, and take your driving licence if you want a motorboat.

Not surprisingly waterskiing is another sport well established here, following so to speak in the motorboat's wake. Indeed the Italian lakes might almost have been specially created for beginners at this exciting pastime. With hardly any waves, and plenty of room on the water, conditions are perfect for getting people quickly on to their feet. Instruction is readily available in any of the larger centres — for more details write to the Italian Water-Ski Association (*Federazione Italiana Sci Nautico*, 44 Via Piranesi, 20137 Milan).

Sailboarding and bathing

There is perhaps less sailboarding than you might expect, although the neighbouring Lake Garda has become a real mecca for this popular sport. Maybe its mass appeal is out of keeping with the more exclusive and individualistic ambience of Lombardy's lakes. Or maybe the explanation lies more with the gentle breezes which blow across the water, too light to keep the sailboarder upright or to offer much in the way of fun.

What then about a refreshing swim in the lakes? Go ahead, they are mostly pretty safe and clean. Virtually all the sewage from the surrounding towns and lakeside communities now goes into treatment plants, and water quality in the lakes has quickly been restored. There are still of course the countless motorboats spewing out their petrol and oil, but at least so far the vast quantities of water swirling about in Lake Como and Lake Maggiore have absorbed the spillage without the balance having been upset. Still, the odd streak of rainbow-coloured petrol will sometimes be encountered as you swim along. And don't expect fine sand on the shore either. The beaches are mostly of coarse sand and pebbles, and the banks drop away steeply into the lake. Some people may find that a swim can be enjoyed with greater ease and comfort in one of the beautiful lakeside pools where the water is kept chlorinated and clear. In the southern half of Lake Como in particular, luxurious swimming pools on terraces built above the level of the lake provide excellent carefree bathing. Even the pampered upper-class Milanese temporarily forsake their summer villas on the hillsides to patronise these lidos.

A paradise for anglers and canoeists

The lakes are so well stocked with fish, all apparently bent on taking the bait, that an angler's pulse cannot help but quicken. More than twenty different kinds of fish including trout, carp, dace, char, tench, eel and pike dart about in the watery vastness of Lake Como. A licence issued by the relevant provincial authority is needed however before tempting any of these lacustrine delicacies on to your hook – further helpful information from the Italian Amateur Fishing Association (*Federazione Italiana Pesca Sportiva*, 79 Viale Abruzzi, 20131 Milan).

Keen oarsmen and canoeists will find plenty to enjoy on Lombardy's Rivers Brembo, Oglio and Ticino, as well as on the section of the Adda which flows through the Valtellina. Week-long canoeing expeditions can even be arranged from Milan to the Adriatic coast, following the Naviglio Pavese, the Ticino and the Po.

Tennis, riding, cycling, golf, climbing and walking

On dry land too Lombardy has just about everything an active holidaymaker could want, with facilities to satisfy almost any whim. Tennis-players will find hard and grass courts in virtually every town and village around the lakes – municipal charges, incidentally, are very reasonable.

Riding in Lombardy means the area around Varese and in the Po Valley. The best-known centres are in Lainate, Ca del Ponte, Rovare Ispra, Cremona and Mantua. Hire is by the hour or for the day.

Cycling is a favourite local pastime. Flat stretches of country and a network of almost traffic-free side-roads ensure that pedalling is not all hard work, so this is definitely the place for anyone who fancies carefree cycling among ricefields, olive-groves, cypresses and magnolia trees. Bicycles can be hired in many of the tourist centres.

Snow peaks in northern Lombardy

Lombardy is also, not surprisingly, a mecca for golf. The finest courses are in Monza (27 holes) and in Como province. To enjoy a round on one of the more exclusive courses visit the little towns of Cassina Rizzardi, Menaggio, Carimate, Franciacorta, Monastero di Luvinate or Montorfano. The course at Birago di Camnago near Milan also enjoys an outstanding reputation among golfers.

For many holidaymakers the special attraction of the Italian lakes is their perfect combination of two contrasting features, mountains and water. In the larger mountain resorts north of the lakes guides are on hand to arrange expeditions for beginners and experienced climbers alike. There are also some fascinating cross-country treks through the magnificent nature reserve at the Stilfser Pass (starting from Bormio) as well as through the Malenco Valley. Anyone with competitive instincts can take part in the *Stramilano*, a colourful and popular fun-run held every spring in Milan.

Life in Lombardy

Over the centuries in Lombardy practical skill has always been valued as highly as artistic talent. And who better to illustrate this truth than Leonardo da Vinci? Before he applied to become naval architect to Duke Ludovico Sforza he had already established a reputation as a talented painter in Florence. His letter of application referred mainly to his ability as an inventor of war machines and catapults, his career as a master architect and painter receiving only passing mention at the end. So it was first and foremost the practical Leonardo who was taken into Duke Ludovico's employment as a hydraulic engineer, and only later that Leonardo the artist was commissioned to paint *The Last Supper*. Angelo Giuseppe Roncalli, who became Pope John XXIII, was an equally typical man of Lombardy. Coming from a farming family near Bergamo, as Pope he never lost his down-to-earth realism.

It is this quality of closeness to reality which more than anything else unites the people of Lombardy, whatever differences there may at first sight seem to be, especially between Milan and its rural surroundings. Sophisticated bankers and stockbrokers from the capital may appear to have little in common with wine-growers in the Valtellina, but appearances can be misleading. Many a director of a large Milanese company has had a father or grandfather who stomped through the cowsheds and over the fields in muddy boots! At some point the opportunity must have arisen for the family to move off the land and resettle itself, preferably in Milan. With typical Lombard perseverance, single-mindedness and unflagging enthusiasm for work the family will have made a success of its new way of life, and by a process of gradual transformation will have become Milanese. Occasionally perhaps some of those who have prospered in this way will attempt to disown their rural origins by adopting a veneer of urban superiority, but this mentality is fortunately not common and in any case is not unique to Lombardy.

Despite its industrialisation Lombardy is still also an agricultural region. The provincial Lombard is a sober character who carefully weighs the pros and cons and meets with cautious scepticism the enthusiasms often shown by southerners in every walk of life. These are qualities shared by the city-dweller from Milan. He too is by nature a pragmatist, keeping a firm check on the kind of wishful thinking that can jeopardise success. Like his farming cousin he has little time for dreams.

It is impossible not to become aware that the people of Lombardy, especially the

Milanese, are not exactly loved by their fellow Italians and are sometimes even openly spurned. As well as a certain envy of this unusually successful breed of men, perhaps there is also a failure fully to understand their extraordinary ambition.

Tourism is one of the pillars of the Lombard economy, bringing a lot of money to the region. Hoteliers and restaurateurs, estate agents and boat-builders have all thrived on it. Earnings are good for most of them and the ablest have become millionaires. Nothing more reflects the affluence of which the people are so proud than the high-spiritedness of the local young set, the *jeunesse dorée*, whose amusements during the summer include making a deafening noise racing boats on the lakes. This and study at the University of Milan are just their way of enjoying the benefits of their parents' lucrative interest in the region's 5,500 hotels and pensions.

The unswerving realism of the Lombard people has not come about by chance. It is owed like as not to a history which has seen the Italian peninsula constantly subject to the whim of foreign rule. The native inhabitants could never be sure from one day to the next what the future would bring. For them the priority was always to face the challenge of the present, and that often meant simply finding a way to survive.

Music and festivals

In northern Italy, as in virtually any tourist area in the world, it is only in the rural backwaters that genuine traditions survive relatively unchanged. Elsewhere towns vie with one another to produce the fullest programme of events and to guarantee their visitors continuous amusement and fun. Tourist officials in the resorts can point proudly to beauty competitions, concerts, regattas, motorboat races, galas and receptions. Many resorts go to great lengths to provide entertainment, some even going so far as to publish a calendar at the beginning of the holiday season listing every single festivity planned for the year. In addition to providing normally accurate details of holiday entertainment, these booklets list mainly the folk festivals, though they also have information on cultural events, and music festivals in particular. The latter are always of a very high standard with artists drawn from all over Italy and even from abroad.

Every year in September and October, for example, *Bergamo*, a once impregnable medieval town which is steeped in culture, puts on a veritable feast of music in celebration of its best-known son, the composer Gaetano Donizetti (1797–1848), who conquered the world with his seventy-four operas. This festival also aims to bring his less famous works to the notice of a wider public.

Also of international significance are the piano festivals held in May and June in *Brescia* and *Bergamo*.

Milano d'Estate (Milan in Summer) is the festive highpoint of the Lombard capital's calendar of events. It is intended as much for those Milanese who have stayed in the city as for visitors from abroad. Performances can be enjoyed in the theatres of the Old Town as well as in the great courtyards of the Sforza castle. The bill of fare includes orchestral concerts, solo performances, plays, classical ballet, pop music, and folk music and dance.

While the cultural programme in Milan and the larger provincial towns continues well into October, the holiday resorts concentrate more on the summer months.

Music and festivals 13

An orchestral concert in Cremona

Information is available from provincial tourist offices, travel agents and local government offices in the resorts.

Festivals are definitely for celebration

For all that they are ambitious and hard working, the people of Lombardy are not at all averse to enjoying life. Festivals are definitely for celebration, and are joyously observed as and when they occur. And they seem in fact to occur pretty often, so that it would be quite impossible to list all the occasions given over to exuberant merrymaking. The following are merely a few highlights. In *Milan* a big festival takes place at the beginning of June in the picturesque Navigli quarter. In May, *Legnano* remembers the famous battle of 1176 in which Barbarossa was defeated by the Lombards; a procession in period costume is held there. In *Curtatone*, near Mantua, folk artists from all over Europe gather on August 15th to create, in coloured chalk on the pavement, splendid pictures of the Virgin Mary.

Italians take it for granted that during the summer months people will live it up until well into the night, and around the lakes in particular there is no limit to the nightlife. Although the discothèques and clubs, bars and pubs have not run riot in quite the same uncontrolled manner as on the beaches of the Adriatic for example, the opportunities for entertainment into the early hours are extremely varied. Here again responsibility rests mainly with the well-heeled youngsters from Milan or Turin who come every summer and turn night into day.

Signposts of history

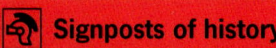

6th c. BC: The Etruscans settle in the Po Valley.

5th c: The Celts arrive, replacing the Etruscans.

3rd/2nd c: Northern Italy comes under Roman domination.

89 BC: Cisalpine Gaul is incorporated into the Roman Empire and flourishes under the Pax Romana, the peace imposed by Roman rule.

AD 293: During the restructuring of the Roman Empire under Diocletian, Milan becomes the seat of the joint-emperor Maximian.

End of the 6th c: The Langobards (Lombards) conquer northern Italy. Pavia becomes their capital in 572.

774: Under Charlemagne the Lombard Empire in northern Italy becomes part of the Frankish Empire.

9th/10th c: Rome is in continuous conflict with the German emperors.

1093: The cities of northern Italy unite in the 'Lombard League' against the Emperor Henry IV.

1118–1128: The cities of Lombardy wage war on independent Como. By defeating Como Milan becomes the most powerful city state in Lombardy.

1154–1177: Emperor Frederick I Barbarossa fails to subdue the Lombard cities. In 1162 Milan is sacked. In 1176 the cities defeat the Emperor at Legnano. At the Peace of Constance (1183) Frederick is finally forced to acknowledge the right of the cities to independence.

1237: Frederick II defeats the cities of northern Italy but then loses all his acquisitions at the Battle of Parma (1248).

13th/14th c: In Milan first the Visconti family and later the Sforza family seek to unify the divided region.

Around 1500: Northern Italy is divided into a number of independent states. In Italy the Renaissance reaches its peak. Austria and France aspire to annex the disunited north.

1701–1714: During the War of Spanish Succession the whole of Lombardy falls to Austria following Prince Eugène's victory at Turin.

1796: Lombardy and Liguria are conquered by Napoleon Bonaparte.

1805: Napoleon is crowned king of Italy in Milan.

1815: The old order is restored under the Congress of Vienna and Austrian hegemony is re-established in Italy. As Lombardo-Venetia Milan and Venice become a province of the Austrian kingdom.

1859: With the aid of Napoleon III the Austrians are driven out of Lombardy.

1860: Italy becomes unified.

1866: Prussia defeats Austria. Austria surrenders all her Italian possessions. For the first time Italian soil is free from foreign troops.

1922: Benito Mussolini creates a fascist state in Italy, beginning a period of oppression.

1943: Italy, on the German side in the Second World War, agrees a cease-fire with the Allied armies. In 1945 Italian partisans capture Mussolini and shoot him near Tremezzo on Lake Como.

1946: Italy becomes a republic.

1970: First regional elections in Lombardy and formation of a regional government based in Milan.

Phases of history

The first inhabitants of northern Italy were an Indo-European people called the *Veneti* and it is through them that something is known of the history of the area from about 1000 BC. In the 6th c. BC the Veneti found their peace disturbed by the Etruscans who pushed northwards, founding cities and engaging in trade with the Greek colonies in southern Italy. One of the Etruscan settlements was called *Melpum*.

Hardly had the Etruscans established themselves, however, when they in turn were overpowered. During the 5th and 4th c. Celtic tribes, the Gauls in particular, made more and more frequent incursions into the region, and finding the Po Valley and lands north of it to their liking, decided to stay. In 396 BC the *Insubres*, a particularly war-like tribe, made short work of Melpum, razing it to the ground. Ever more emboldened they embarked on a campaign of hostilities which took them as far south as Rome. They had clearly not taken the Romans into their calculations, however. The Roman army fought back and little by little brought northern Italy under Roman domination. Melpum was captured in 222 BC and became *Mediolanum*, the future Milan. Elsewhere there were further breathtaking advances, military bases were established, and within thirty years the *Boii*, last of the still-defiant Celtic tribes, had been subdued, which completed the conquest of Cisalpine Gaul – the part of Gaul which lay on the Rome side of the Alps.

In 49 BC the whole of this former region of Gaul was under the governorship of Julius Caesar. Mediolanum, Vicetia (Vicenza), Brixia (Brescia), Mantua and Verona were among a number of increasingly influential cities and military bases whose inhabitants by then enjoyed Roman citizenship. Caesar, however, had greater ambitions. Crossing the Rubicon near Rimini at the head of an army he marched on Rome. Fast on his heels came the overthrow of the Roman Republic.

From the Roman Empire to the Frankish Empire

The period of Roman imperialism which followed the demise of the Republic brought peace and prosperity. What were once military camps evolved into thriving cities. Christianity spread quickly following the Emperor Constantine's declaration of tolerance in the Edict of Milan, bishoprics springing up all over Italy. Among the most important was Milan, raised to spiritual pre-eminence by St Ambrose (339–397), one of the four Fathers of the Church.

This calm was followed by a series of storms. In the first place the Roman Empire was divided into East and West, with Ravenna becoming the (last) capital of the Western Empire. Then came invasion by Germanic tribes very much fiercer and more resolute than their Gallic predecessors. The Huns led by Attila rampaged through northern Italy killing and burning, sacking Milan in 452.

Zeno, the emperor in the East, now tried to save the Western Empire. In 493 with his support Theodoric the Great, king of the Ostrogoths, overthrew the German chieftain Odoacer to become ruler in the West.

Towards the end of the 6th c. it was the turn of yet another belligerent tribe to surge down across the Alps. In next to no time these newcomers, the Lombards, had swept aside everyone in their path. They at first tried to rule their territories from Verona but soon made Pavia the capital of their empire in northern Italy. Later, made bold by their success and greedy for further conquests, they threatened Rome itself. The Pope in desperation called upon the Franks for help.

Charlemagne answered the call, defeating Desiderius, last of the 8th c. Lombard kings. In an attempt to secure his hold on the region Charlemagne had his son Pepin crowned king of Italy. Even so Frankish rule soon collapsed following Charlemagne's death.

The rise of the north Italian cities

Over the next few centuries Italy was bled by a series of disputes between the papacy and the German emperors. A state of permanent conflict ensued developing into long-term stalemate with neither side able to gain the upper hand. There could have been no better political climate for the cities. Here at last was the long-sought-after opportunity to fight for rights and independence, and to build up their economic strength. City republics mushroomed everywhere, the stronger to survive, the weaker to disappear as quickly as they had arisen. Commerce prospered. Merchants and tradesmen made huge fortunes. The old economic order was gradually replaced by a monetary economy. Altogether it was one of the decisive stages in the development of the West. Venice became immensely rich and consequently began to establish trading links with the eastern Mediterranean, Byzantium and the Levant. The cities of northern Italy became staging posts on the routes to northern and western Europe, from where they also received goods traded in return. While thus playing the roles of middlemen and distributors they also became producers on their own account, processing some of the traded materials themselves. People responded swiftly to the new developments. An enlarged canal network and efficient system of canal management provided the cheapest transport, so facilitating the movement of goods.

Almost at once a completely new professional class emerged within the flourishing cities – the judges and notaries, most of whom came from the nobility. Their services were needed because people's rights and also conditions of ownership remained obscure in these city republics that had sprung up so quickly. It is clear from their enormous numbers that they were much in demand. There are assumed to have been about 2,000 notaries in Bologna, about 1,500 in Milan and about 600 in Padua at the end of the 13th c. Legal studies, not surprisingly, became one of the leading disciplines at Italian universities.

Larger purses it seems encouraged larger families. At any rate the population almost doubled compared with that in the 10th c. It is estimated that at the end of the 13th c. a medium-sized town in northern Italy had about 20,000 inhabitants. There were numerous smaller communities of between 5,000 and 10,000, and some very large ones for the period, with as many as 50,000 city-dwellers.

When in the 14th c. the city states of northern Italy lost their independence, this was far from being the end of their cultural flowering. The rulers under whose control they fell often proved to be generous and enlightened patrons of the arts. But it was not only the rulers who preserved the heritage of the cities and continued to give to every kind of intellectual and artistic activity the kind of support it had long enjoyed; their example was followed by the ordinary townspeople too.

Foreign rulers in a rich land

At the beginning of the 18th c., during the War of Spanish Succession, a brave man won a great battle and as a result the whole of Lombardy changed hands. The man in question was the aristocratic general Prince Eugène who, following the siege of Turin, made Austria the new mistress of northern Italy. The end of the century saw the arrival of Napoleon Bonaparte. He overran Lombardy and Liguria, subsequently proclaiming himself king of Italy in Milan. For a time whole kingdoms and provinces were shuttled backwards and forwards like pieces on a chessboard. In the end the European powers lured the Corsican into check, as it were. Napoleon was toppled and the victors celebrated at the Congress of Vienna. The Austrian emperor became sovereign of the newly created kingdom of Lombardo-Venetia.

As described by a correspondent of *The Times*, conditions were prosperous under Habsburg rule. The land, he recorded, was richer than ever it could be in a free Italy, though this apparently did little to endear the Austrians to the native inhabitants. The more affluent Italy's nobility and middle class became the more they hankered after the forbidden fruits of political power instead of 'only grazing like sheep and fattening themselves on the green meadows of the Fatherland'. The entire urban population was united in wanting to be freed from the ubiquitous and alien policing of the Austrians.

Calls for a new, politically active order grew ever louder, with protest being felt most evidently in Milan – but not only there. The desire for speedy change brought widespread discontent. This after all was a highly creative time in Italy; there was a feeling in the air that there were great things to accomplish. Artists, musicians and writers were more productive than they had been for 300 years. Even though the music of Rossini and Verdi and the novels of Alessandro Manzoni were only indirectly political, they nevertheless helped to cement a sense of national identity. In drawing-rooms and on the streets all agreed on the need for change, the need to bring political reality and ideas into harmony. But what exactly did that mean? The oppressed Italians differed in their views.

Should a unified Italian republic be created, or a unified Italian monarchy; a confederation of republican states, or a number of kingdoms presided over by the pope? Idea after idea circulated, each with its adherents. The single demand shared by every patriot was that the Austrians must go. In the spring of 1848 anger against the Austrians spilled over. The Habsburg monarchy was tottering in Europe, adrift and directionless, a rudderless ship. Now in Italy all hell broke loose. The people took to the streets in an explosion of impassioned political energy. The Milanese were first to rebel. The Austrian commander-in-chief Radetzky was forced to withdraw his troops to the safety of the 'Quadrilateral', a square of forts in the Po Valley. Venice was declared a republic. The king of Sardinia-Piedmont sent an army to assist the insurgent Lombards, and help came also from Naples and from papal Rome. For one brief moment the whole of Italy was abuzz with talk of revolution – no matter whether war had been formally declared on the Habsburgs or not.

The Austrians however regained their composure. At the head of a well-drilled peasant militia, commanders with experience of military operations in northern Italy recaptured Lombardy and put down the Piedmontese. French troops, on whom the hopes of the Italian revolutionaries rested, were put to flight, and an Austrian victory was assured. It was a victory for arms, and though it proved sufficient to seal the fate of central Europe for another decade it left the Italian question far from solved. It was Napoleon III who made the first move towards a decisive resolution. With his help the Austrians were finally driven from Lombardy in 1859.

For the art-lover

Traces of every cultural epoch are etched deep in the nine provinces of Lombardy. The very earliest activity is evidenced around the lakes of northern Italy where the oldest of all the region's art has been discovered – drawings and inscriptions carved in the rocks of the Camonica Valley almost as if frozen in time. Near Como there are remains of some ancient settlements which offer a glimpse into life in Gaul. The museums at Pavia, Brescia and Mantua all have collections of artefacts dating from pre-Roman times. The Romans of course left a rich legacy everywhere they went, but who would have expected to find in Brescia a Capitoline temple built by Vespasian?

The independent spirit of Lombard art is at its most obvious in the Middle Ages. Here, particularly in the region's many little churches, of which there are fine examples in Pavia, Como and Milan, is work so expressive as to equal the best in southern Europe. In the 8th and 9th c. Milan also acquired a reputation for enamelwork. The city's talented artists were almost certainly responsible for the Iron Crown of Lombardy, now in Monza Cathedral. Kings of Italy were crowned with it from medieval times; Napoleon (in 1805) and Ferdinand I (in 1838) were the last.

The Lombard period

To talk of a 'Lombard period' beginning around the turn of the millennium is far from an idle boast. The *maestri Comacini* were architects of world rank whose style and technological expertise were to have an effect across the whole of Europe. Even so they had rivals in the *Intelvesi*, master church-builders from the Intelvi valley who used brick both as a building material and for decoration. They applied their techniques first to the decoration of churches, later to the towers of civic buildings, and in the end to castles and villas.

Then the Gothic style came to Lombardy and buildings had to be of marble and quarried natural stone. The results are plain to see in the Piazza Vecchia in Bergamo, one of the most impressive of all late medieval squares.

Piazza Vecchia in Bergamo

Milan Cathedral

Between the Gothic and Renaissance periods art in Lombardy gained a new vigour. It was then that the noted Lombard school of miniature-painting and decoration blossomed. Giotto, Pisanello, Alberti, Bramante, Tiepolo and of course Leonardo da Vinci were among the famous artists who gave inspiration to the times.

Flourishing too was the 15th c. Lombard school of sculptors. They attacked their stone with such enthusiasm that they achieved a hitherto unequalled quality of expressiveness, some of the finest examples of which can be seen in the charterhouse at Pavia and the cathedral in Milan.

Villas and palaces of the 18th century

In stark contrast to earlier periods architecture in Lombardy generally lacked distinction throughout the age of Baroque. By this time all the north Italian painters of distinction were gathered in Milan and architecture was thoroughly eclipsed by painting.

In the 18th c., however, eloquent examples of Late Baroque appeared, especially in Milan. There followed a gradual transition to Italian Rococo. The wealth of Lombardy was now devoted to building on a grand scale. In the capital, in Brescia, Cremona and Varese, in the Varesotto, but most of all around the lakes, a string of magnificent villas and palaces appeared, blended into a landscape of almost tropical luxuriance.

Thereafter a succession of poets, musicians and writers were drawn to Lombardy, mostly to the lakes: Flaubert and Stendhal, Verdi, Bellini, Liszt and Kafka. Even if they didn't settle there, a spark of inspiration surely passed into their work as the result of each visit to this earthly paradise.

Food and drink

No problems with the food here! Just sit down and enjoy the delights of the regional cooking. In contrast to the seaside promenades of the Adriatic you will find no British-style pubs, and you will search in vain for menus geared specifically to the tourist trade. Lombard restaurateurs know full well that their tourist patrons are keen to savour the area's rich variety of dishes rather than be offered the same old familiar food from home which might be chosen purely out of laziness. Lombardy in fact is a gourmet's paradise with some of the best and most varied cuisine in the whole of Italy.

Trattoria or osteria?

It's important in Italy to know about the different kinds of restaurants. A *ristorante* is an expensive, well-appointed restaurant which will satisfy even the most exacting requirements. Its cuisine will be of international standard, but equally it is likely to make some concessions to the rather stereotyped tastes of the European jet set. Regional specialities will be offered along with other dishes but will not usually be given pride of place.

Trattorie are quite different. Furnished more simply than a ristorante and offering good, mainly reasonably priced food typical of the region, the trattoria is where the local people tend to eat.

Rosticcerie, mainly found in the large cities, are different again. They are good for quick snacks and also serve take-away food. Hardly a speciality of any particular region, *pizzerie* will be familiar to almost everyone. They are found in all Italian holiday resorts. They are usually comfortably furnished, and use wood-stoves for the cooking. Pizzas are now on the menu at many ristoranti too.

An *osteria* is an unpretentious sort of wine bar to which you can bring your own food without anyone looking askance.

Wherever you go in Italy it is soon obvious that the *bar* is one of life's necessities. But Italian bars mean *cappuccino, espresso* and fresh *cornetti* at breakfast time, and sandwiches, alcoholic drinks, newspapers and conversation throughout the day. Patronised primarily by the locals with hardly a tourist in sight, the bar has an atmosphere which is quite special and thoroughly stimulating – as artists and writers have long since found.

Lombardy's culinary delights

There can be few people luckier than the Lombards when it comes to having good food growing on the doorstep. There is simply everything. The Po Valley produces the finest rice; cattle and pigs thrive on the rich pastures, and fat trout dart in the gushing mountain streams. The region is also famous for its poultry. Fertile land stretching all the way from the foothills of the Alps far into the lowland plain means an inexhaustible abundance of different kinds of vegetables and, of course, fruit. As a result the tables of every province of Lombardy carry delicious surprises for the gourmet holidaymaker.

Some Lombard specialities such as *risotto, Milan cutlets, minestrone* (vegetable soup) and *panettone* (the now familiar Christmas cake) have proved so delectable to the widely indulged Italian palate that they have been taken up by cooks throughout the length and breadth of Italy, as far south even as Sicily. In contrast other regional dishes are to be had only in speciality restaurants or in small country inns.

Provincial specialities

In the province of Bergamo the *polenta* (similar to semolina but made with maize meal) served with cheese, mushrooms or quail is excellent, as is *taleggio*, a typical local cheese. In nearby Brescia large stuffed envelopes of pasta called *canonsei* are a particular favourite. The *salami* here is especially good too; it deserves a place in any picnic basket and makes an ideal snack to take on a long walk. Before leaving Brescia be sure to sample the deliciously tasty *salmon trout* from Lake Iseo.

Between Milan and Bergamo is the home of a world-famous cheese bearing the name of the little town from which it comes: *Gorgonzola*. According to the experts, only cows which graze on certain pastures produce milk suitable for making it. The manufacturing process is simple in the extreme with a natural mould developing as the curds are aerated using a piece of copper wire. The cheese itself forms in next to no time but the real skill is in seeing that it ripens properly, the important thing being to maintain the correct low temperature. Incidentally, no Italian would eat Gorgonzola in the advanced state of ripeness insisted on by some foreign connoisseurs. The ripening period for a Gorgonzola destined for the Italian market is only two months, compared with three and a half months for many foreign markets.

In Cremona try *marubini*, another kind of pasta envelope. Anyone with a sweet tooth should also be sure to sample the *torroni*, honey and almond sticks which are heavenly eaten with a cup of espresso coffee. In the neighbouring province of Mantua there are *tortelli di zucca*, pasta envelopes with a sweet filling. *Agnolini* is another Mantua speciality, small ravioli prepared in a particularly delicious way and served in a meat broth. And how about some *Mantua garlic sausage*? Also definitely worth trying are *grana cheese* (a kind of Parmesan) and *sbrisolona*, an almond cake.

Frogs fried or braised, the favourite dish in Pavia province, are not to everyone's liking. But if that particular speciality doesn't appeal to you the province has plenty more to offer. There is a choice of fish from the River Ticino, mushrooms from the Oltrepò, goose sausage from Mortara, salami from Varzi, *offelle* (butter biscuits) from Parona, and *torta paradiso* (a cake) from the town of Pavia itself.

Next on any gourmet's itinerary must be the province of Sondrio. Here the specialities include *pizzoccheri* (buckwheat noodles prepared with butter, cheese and vegetables), *polenta taragna* (with spicy *bitto cheese*), *breasola* (a kind of smoked meat) and *sciatt* (a pancake with a cheese filling).

In Varese province you can sample the tastiest of asparagus while from Saronno come the famous *amaretti*, biscuits made from bitter almonds.

It should be clear by now that this is a region where every palate is catered for. In virtually any trattoria or osteria you can also sample all the different ways of preparing risotto. Naturally the Lombards know better than anyone how to prepare it; they have been cultivating rice for centuries. The choice is yours. You can have prawns and rice, chicken liver and rice, squid and rice, quail and rice, spinach and rice, or *risi bisi* (rice and young peas, an excellent spring dish).

Now a word about Milan which has a gastronomic culture deserving a chapter all on its own. In comparison with that of other major Italian cities the food in Milan is certainly above average. The art of Italian cooking with all its nuances is well represented here, from the imaginative interpretations of nouvelle cuisine to substantial peasant dishes from southern Italy.

A sign above a trattoria saying *cucina casalinga* means that the proprietress does the cooking herself. Most restaurants in Lombardy are family businesses and this means that food is always freshly prepared. In this culinary Utopia almost everything is of the best and made with butter.

Two typical recipes from Lombardy

Polenta incassata (polenta with meat sauce)

This recipe (for six people) reflects the Lombard partiality for substantial dishes containing many ingredients. The best polenta is made by pouring maize meal into lightly salted boiling water, stirring continuously. The precise quantity of meal is a matter of personal taste, but also depends on the type of maize used; different qualities absorb larger or smaller amounts of water. In Lombardy polènta is always on the firm side. It is ready when it falls away from the side of the saucepan. Spread it out on a flat surface and cut into not too thick slices.

Next prepare a large quantity of meat sauce together with a béchamel sauce made with a pint of milk.

For the meat sauce chop and then brown an onion, a carrot, celery and 50 g of belly of pork. Add 300 g of lean beef cut into small cubes and 150 g of chicken liver, also cut up small. Brown for five minutes and add a glass of red wine. Just before all the wine has evaporated stir in 500 g of fresh, peeled tomatoes and season with salt and pepper. Pour on a meat stock and leave to cook for forty minutes on a low heat.

For the béchamel sauce first heat a pint of milk. In another saucepan melt 50 g of butter and stir in 30 g of flour together with salt, pepper and nutmeg. Gradually mix in the hot milk and continue cooking for about ten minutes, stirring all the time to avoid lumps.

Now layer the slices of polenta and the meat and béchamel sauces in an oven-proof dish, sprinkling each layer with Parmesan cheese. A large quantity of meat sauce is needed since the polenta will absorb a considerable amount. Bake the whole thing in a hot oven for about half an hour and then serve straight away.

Ossobuco (braised knuckle of veal)

This is a dish typical of the Milan area. For four people: cut half an onion, a stick of celery and a carrot into cubes and chop a bunch of parsley. Sweat in 50 g of butter. Lightly flour four slices (4 cm thick) of knuckle of pork with the marrow still in the bone and fry until golden brown. Add a few sage leaves, a glass of dry white wine and, if required, a pinch of salt. While the wine is evaporating, gradually pour in a few ladlefuls of clear stock to prevent the pieces of knuckle from drying up. Cook for about one hour. Serve very hot in its own juices.

Food and drink 23

A vineyard in northern Italy

Dry red wine matures in a Lombardy wine cellar

And a pretty good drop of wine!

Around the Italian lakes and in Milan drinking-habits are the same as in the rest of Italy, which means that wine is drunk at meals, regularly, in moderation, and almost to the exclusion of anything else. The local wines *(vino della casa)*, which tend to be light, dry and easily digested, are served everywhere. Prices are reasonable and away from the major centres are often remarkably low.

The wine cellars of Lombardy stock thirty-three brands of wine under a label which guarantees its origin and quality. The wine is mainly cultivated in three areas, the Oltrepò Pavese, the Valtellina and the Franciacorta district. Driving around looking for the wine co-operatives in particular villages or for growers who sell their wine directly to the public provides a good opportunity to become acquainted with the scenic charm of the area and to discover its good food.

Many famous varieties of grapes grow in the vineyards on the gentle, undulating hills of the Oltrepò, from the Po Valley to Monte Penice and the Brallo Pass. Among the red wines are *Barbera, Bonardo, Barbacarlo, Buttafuoco, Rosso dell'Oltrepò* and *Sangue di Giuda*. *Buttafuoco* is a dry red wine, unfortunately often served too warm. If you like strong red wines try the *Barbacarlo*. It is full-bodied with a good, rich bouquet and a slightly raised alcohol content. In good years it resembles a medium Burgundy. White wines include *Riesling, Pinot bianco* and *Cortese*. Dry and generally excellent sparkling wines and sweet, bubbling Muscatels are further palate-ticklers from this area.

The Valtellina produces mainly robust red wines such as *Sassella, Grumello, Inferno, Valtellina Rosso, Valgella* and *Sforzato*, most of which can be laid down for several years.

The Franciacorta district is renowned for its superb champagne, almost as good as the French variety. It is also the home of two very popular wines, *Franciacorta Rosso* (red) and *Franciacorta Pinot* (white).

Other wines to have made a name for themselves among connoisseurs are *Lugana* and *Tocai di San Martino* (both white) which come from Brescia province, and *Valcalepio* (of which there are red and white varieties) from the area between Bergamo and Lake Iseo. Lastly, from the province of Mantua comes *Colli Morenici Mantovani* (red, rosé and white).

Something worth keeping in mind: heat and alcohol don't always go too well together. Remember also that in some restaurants when wine is ordered it is customary to put a whole bottle on the table but to charge only for the amount actually consumed. A good idea is to follow the example of the Italians themselves who know how to avoid coming to grief when drinking wine, and how to keep it a pleasure. As well as wine they order a bottle of fizzy *(gasata)* or still *(naturale)* mineral water *(acqua minerale)*. The waiter will automatically bring extra glasses so that the two need not be mixed.

Fresh fruit in the market

Shopping

Italy's high inflation rate has all but put an end to its reputation as the shopper's paradise south of the Alps. Nowadays the saying that everything is cheap in Italy amounts to little more than idle talk, especially in relation to the area around the Italian lakes. The legendary Italian shoes and leather goods are scarcely more expensive in London than in Padua or Milan. Of course holiday shopping involves a rather special frame of mind. Who after all counts the cost when confronted with a useful – or even just a pretty – memento to be taken home from a holiday in another country? In Lombardy there is nothing easier than finding things to spend your money on. Milan, don't forget, is renowned the world over as a centre of fashion. Together with the adjacent area the Via Monte Napoleone and Via della Spiga are its most elegant but at the same time its most expensive shopping streets. For a large selection of goods at more affordable prices go to the Corso Buenos Aires.

Como is famous for its silk fabrics and scarves which make exquisite presents for those at home.

The largest selection of shoes is to be found in Vigevano, Varese and Parabiago. In the Brianza district north of Milan there are a number of furniture factories which export their products all over the world. The choice covers furniture in every style and to suit every purse.

In Stradivari's home town Cremona it is still possible to buy one of his world-famous violins, though it will cost a fortune. Stradivari, without question the world's most accomplished violin-maker, was born in 1644. He died in 1737 aged ninety-three. It is claimed that in his seventy-year working life he made 1,116 violins, violas and cellos, an average of sixteen instruments a year. He is said to have once told one of his pupils: 'None of you will ever make a better violin than I.'

For anyone wanting to buy an accordion Stradella is the place to go. In Goito, near Mantua, elaborate articles are handcrafted in tin (the prices are right for the quality so you can buy with confidence here). Wood carvings are typical of the area around Bergamo while in the Valtellina you can buy *pezzotti*, handwoven country-style carpets.

Among the large weekly markets where almost everything – including good clothes – can be found, the Wednesday market at Luino on Lake Maggiore and the Como Saturday market are especially alluring. As everyone will probably appreciate, whereas the larger shops mostly have fixed prices the market is the place for bargaining. Frequent use should be made of the word *sconto* (discount) in any dealings with market traders!

And here's another tip: don't have anything to do with 'antiques'. A sensational discovery is exceedingly unlikely – the chances of finding an original chest from a Sforza palace in some little provincial shop must be at most one in a million!

Hints for your holiday

The Italians are sometimes thought of as a really 'laid-back', happy-go-lucky, informal people, but they work extremely hard, and while they may admittedly be slightly less conservative than people north of the Alps, foreign visitors should be aware that it is not the case that 'anything goes'. Brief bikinis are of course fine on the beach, but you will rarely see a scantily clad Italian woman on a shopping trip in the centre of town and never see one visiting a church in a low-cut sun-dress. Similarly there is very little topless sunbathing in Lombardy, and drunken behaviour after an intoxicating evening in an osteria is very much the exception. You will probably find yourself welcomed at your holiday destination by an easy-going, relaxed and carefree people who may nevertheless be tactful and reserved in conversation. Except, that is, as far as your children are concerned – the Italians' love of children is well known.

Ascona on Lake Maggiore's western shore

Where to go and what to see

Lake Maggiore

Lake Maggiore is 194 m above sea-level and is deepest between Ghiffa and Porto Valtravaglia where a sounding of 372 m has been recorded. Counting the Gulf of Borromeo the lake measures 12 km at its widest point. At its narrowest near Arona, on the other hand, only 2 km separates the two shores. With a total surface area of 212 sq km it is the second largest lake in the pre-Alps of northern Italy. It also has more islands than any other lake in northern Italy. In winter the average temperature scarcely ever falls below 5°C/41°F and in summer it seldom rises above 27°C/81°F.

The rivers Maggia and Ticino (called the Tessin in Switzerland) feed Lake Maggiore from the north while the Toce flows into the Gulf of Borromeo from the west. The Ticino flows out of the lake again at its southern end.

Anyone looking closely at Lake Maggiore will soon see that none of the lakeside survives in its natural state. It has been moulded, shaped and built upon by man, though not over-built or spoiled. It has not fallen prey to large-scale development or towering concrete. With the exception of one or two architectural 'blunders' scenic harmony still reigns on the lake today as it did a hundred years ago.

Towards the southern end of the big lake, almost within hailing distance so to speak, are its smaller sister-lakes, Lago di Varese, Lago di Comabbio and Lago di Monate to the east, Lago di Mergozzo and Lake Orta to the west. All are worth an excursion at any time, though not all are suitable for bathing (more about that later).

Lake Maggiore: the eastern shore

The eastern shore
Luino Pop. 15,000

Luino, largest and unquestionably also most elegant of all the towns on the lake's eastern shore, lies in a broad bay encircled by green, wooded hills. Enthroned above the small harbour is a golden statue of the Madonna. The lakeside promenade is screened by a stupendous avenue of maples, giving it a most impressive grandeur.

Tourism is not the foremost contributor to the council budget in Luino, that honour going to its profitable industries, in particular the textile factories, which provide the town's inhabitants with a good livelihood. But even if the tourist isn't exactly king in Luino, all the ingredients of a perfect holiday can be found here, especially a family holiday. There are reasonable pensions as well as expensive hotels, a first-rate tourist

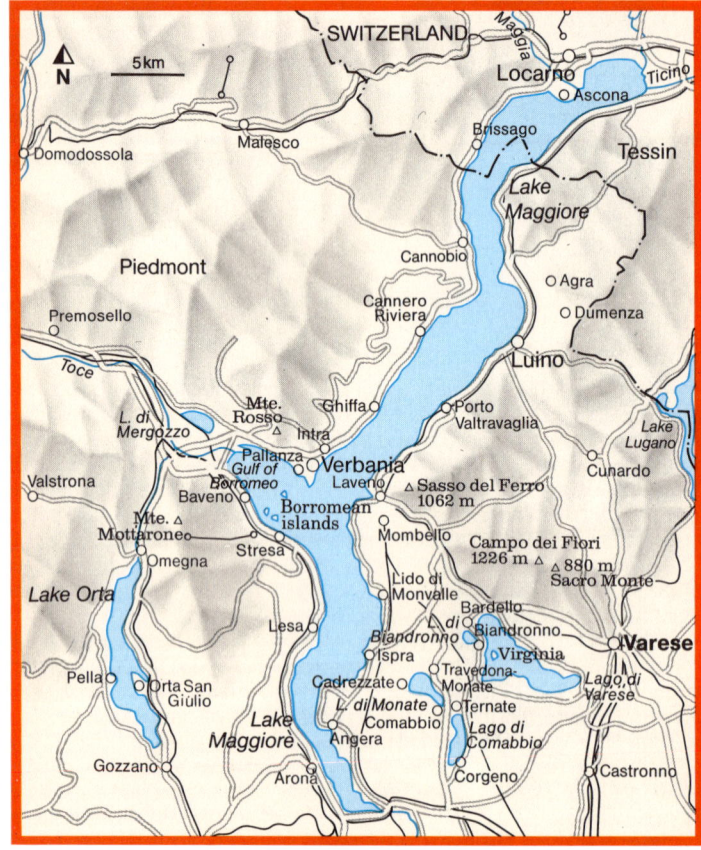

Laveno

office, a natural, albeit pebbly, beach, and opportunities for virtually any watersport the ideal holiday might require. Luino is a thoroughly Italian little town, at its most noisy and colourful on Wednesdays when locals and visitors alike flock to the market.

Concealed behind tall trees on the splendid lakeside promenade stands the church of *Madonna del Carmine*, founded in the 15th c. by the Luino-born Carmelite monk Giacobino Luinese. The frescos in the chapel on the left-hand side of the single-nave church are attributed to pupils of Bernardo Luini, the most important of Lombardy's Renaissance painters. He too was born in Luino and was apparently influenced by Leonardo da Vinci.

Also of note are the *museum* and the *Oratorio di San Pietro* with its frescos.

The beach on the edge of the town is pebbly and drops away steeply into the lake. When the wind is unfavourable the water here is polluted by ferries and motorboats, so showers have been installed.

 Rowing boats and pedalos for hire.

 Motorboat hire.

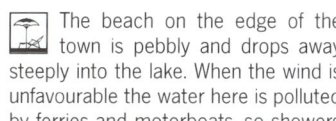

 In the Piazza Garibaldi where there are a number of tiny osterias you can enjoy excellent food at reasonable prices.

Ex **To the mountain valleys**

Tucked away behind Luino are mountain valleys absolutely ideal for walking. It is also possible to drive to most of the mountain villages though some care is required. You can make an excursion, for example, through the *Dumentina Valley* to the mountain village of *Agra*. The drive takes you through the main town in the valley, *Dumenza*, from where there is a fine view of the distant mountains around Lake Lugano.

This is also hippy territory. But it takes money to drop out here — no problem apparently for an Italian count from Milan wanting to buy an abandoned hermitage, renovate it, decorate it with the skulls of cows, paint human skulls on it and fill it with cult music. To avoid being bored while getting back to nature the devotees of the alternative culture gather herbs for infusing into herbal teas and distilling into liqueurs.

Laveno Pop. 9,000

The Roman general Titus Labienus is said to have given this little town its name, though this is by no means certain. The claim that a great battle between the Romans and the Cimbri once took place here may be a good source of publicity but as history it too is rather shaky. Laveno is a homely little holiday resort with a mountain of its very own, the *Sasso del Ferro*. From the peak (1,062 m) the view of the central part of Lake Maggiore is a real feast for the eyes, a pleasure which can be experienced in complete comfort since a cable car runs to the top.

At neighbouring *Cerro*, 3 km

away on a good road, there is a superb collection of ceramics in the *Civica Raccolta di Terraglia* (open 2.30–6 pm, closed Mon., Fri.–Sun. also 10 am–noon).

 Small, stony beach which slopes sharply into the lake.

 Delightful excursions can be made by steamer or by the faster hydrofoil to virtually every town on Lake Maggiore. The trip from Laveno to Locarno at the north end of the lake takes three hours. Two worthwhile spots closer at hand are the pilgrimage church of *Santa Caterina del Sasso* (5 km), which clings to a steep rock above the lake, and the artists' village of *Arcumeggio* (12 km) with its painted façades.

Ispra Pop. 4,200

This peaceful little place owes its fame rather more to its role in the world of science than to its qualities as a holiday resort, with Euratom having constructed a nuclear research centre on the edge of town. Ispra does however have a particular source of appeal for the holidaymaker which makes it an excellent base for watersports, for a little way north of the town is the *Lido di Monvalle*. This flat strip of shoreline, partly overgrown with reeds, is most unusual for Lake Maggiore because you tread not on shingle or stones but on sand. The sandy beach here is in fact the most spacious of all the bathing places on the lake.

Angera Pop. 5,500

A village on the shores of a hilly promontory. The Romans called the settlement Vicus Sebuinus and turned it into a fortified trading harbour.

 The church and the fortress

The church at the end of the long, shady lakeside promenade is *Madonna di Riva* (Our Lady of the Shore). Inside on the left hangs a huge painting by Camillo Procaccini (1551–1629) depicting a scene from the life of the saint Charles Borromeo. Even today the Borromeo are a leading family on Lake Maggiore; for five centuries they have been in possession of the major attraction on the lake's eastern shore, the *Rocca di Angera* (open from the end of March to the end of October, 9.30 am–12.30 pm and 2–6 pm). The fortress is 2 km from the centre of the village along a well-signposted road. You can easily walk there or you can take the car.

Especially worth seeing in the interior of the mighty fortress are the frescos by Michelino da Besozzo (1388–1442), and the Doll Museum. The Gothic courtroom with its cross-vaulting is interesting from an architectural point of view and also has early 14th c. frescos very reminiscent of the Byzantine style.

The Angera fortress is an impressive example of a feature which is peculiar to Lake Maggiore. In the Middle Ages a great number of castles and towers kept watch over the lake, their purpose being to maintain control of the roads and footpaths on both sides. A system of beacons stationed within sight of each other ensured by means of fire and smoke signals that Milan received early warning of any danger of attack.

The fortresses of Angera and Arona, facing one another across Lake Maggiore at its narrowest point, represented an insurmountable obstacle to medieval weaponry.

Lake Maggiore: the eastern shore

 A special tip
A visit to the fortress at Angera offers more than just a lesson in history. From spring right through to autumn there are superbly arranged exhibitions of work by internationally acclaimed contemporary artists. To do everything justice will take at least half a day. The special charm of these exhibitions soon makes itself felt: the modern paintings are displayed in centuries-old, lofty rooms whose walls are made from huge blocks of stone. The lancet windows give a fine view of the lake at the same time as drawing into the rooms and on to the pictures the fresh, clear light reflected from the water.

And there is something else. The fortress is surrounded on three sides by vineyards. Here choice vines are cultivated to produce the well-known *Vino della Rocca di Angera*.

The Varesotto lakes
Driving north from Angera a turn-off to the right after about 6 km takes you through Cadrezzate to *Lago di Monate*.

Lago di Monate
The countryside around the tranquil lake is an absolute picture, full of meadows and woodland. The smallest of the three Varesotto lakes, Monate is barely 3 km long and 1 km wide. Don't expect holiday development with all the associated infrastructure; at most there are one or two campsites dotted about (Italians living not too far away come here at summer weekends to bathe). The local people quietly pursue their own way of life, not at all resentful it seems at having to play second fiddle to the big lakes with their lively tourist resorts.

Travedona-Monate Pop. 3,000
This little town is not a place to spend a whole holiday, but it definitely repays a visit. It has the air of a mountain village in some remote corner of the Tyrol: tiny, narrow alleyways, old houses built of grey, weathered granite, an occasional dog roaming around the quiet little streets, and a small parish church with 14th c. frescos. Time seems to be at a standstill.

Lago di Comabbio
Drive via Comabbio to Ternate, at the north end of Lake Comabbio. Although parts of the road are in poor condition it is nevertheless worth continuing south along the eastern shore to *Corgeno* from where you can get a view over the whole of the lake. In good visibility it is possible to see as far as the Alps. Lago di Comabbio is about the same size as Lago di Monate. There are limited sporting facilities at both lakes.

 Shingle beach descending gently into the lake; clean water in most parts.

Lago di Varese
Heading north towards Bardello, you pass *Lago di Biandronno* on the left-hand side. There is really nothing to stop for here; what was once the lake is now little more than a fishpond overgrown with reeds.

Lago di Varese, 8.5 km by 4.5 km, is beautifully situated. Unfortunately it is a delight only to the eye. Over the last few decades pollution by industrial waste and sewage from nearby towns has made the water turbid, de-oxygenating the lower layers. Although treatment plants have been built in an attempt to revitalise the waters, they still have not

Lake Maggiore: the eastern shore

Sunset over Lago di Varese

recovered and to the local fishermen it is little more than a *lago morto*, a dead lake. Bathing is completely banned. In fact there is scarcely any life on the lake at all, just one or two sailing boats and a few fishermen waiting in desperation to see whether the last remaining dace or trout will bite.

Don't let all this deter you though from making the delightful trip out into the middle of the lake to the curious little islet of *Virginia* (it costs only a few lire to be ferried over by motorboat).

A prehistoric pile settlement was discovered here. Scientists have since been able to show that the island itself was formed from refuse left behind by early settlers whose huts once stood above the water on piles. Walking around this tiny dot of land it is as if you are in another world, with cedars of Lebanon, cypresses and rare species of birds for company. Since there tend to be rather few visitors you are treated like royalty in the small restaurant run by the padrone and his daughter.

Varese Pop. 90,000
The city squats like a great spider at the centre of a dense web of roads crisscrossing this heavily populated part of Italy. Varese is not so much a typical holiday town as an extremely active industrial centre. The hotels are used mainly by people travelling on business. It is to its silk industry above all else that Varese owes its fame. The Varesini are hard-working people, on their feet day in, day out on the floors of the big factories which have grown from more modest beginnings as small artisan workshops. In and around this enterprising provincial capital, however, there are quite a number of interesting things that are definitely worth seeing.

In Varese itself two buildings in particular are not to be missed. Standing in the park facing the *city hall* you could be forgiven for thinking you were in Austria rather than Italy. What is now the city hall was formerly the summer and autumn residence of Francis III d'Este, Duke of Modena. As you stroll through the beautifully kept park with the front of the elegant late 18th c. building in full view it is as if the Viennese palace of Schönbrunn stood before you in miniature.

Go through the park and uphill to the left. In a few minutes you reach the *Villa Mirabello*, now the home of the town museum. The Villa is framed by a lovely English-style garden. Prehistoric and other archaeological collections have been brought together here, including finds from the Virginia island site. (Open daily 9.30 am–12.30 pm and 2.30–5.30 pm; public holidays on mornings only.)

On the outskirts of Varese, in *Biumo Superiore*, there are two other magnificent buildings, standing in a large park: the *Villa Fabio Ponte* (17th c.) and the smaller *Villa Andrea Ponti* (18th c.). Both are used today as conference centres.

 Sacro Monte and Campo dei Fiori.
Some 10 km from Varese (about thirty

minutes by car) is a hill known as Sacro Monte, rising to a height of 880 m. With its typically medieval village it makes a popular outing, especially for people with an interest in religious sites. Starting at the *Prima Cappella* there is a steep but extremely impressive path which, in about an hour and a half, takes you past fourteen Lady chapels up to the sanctuary of *Santa Maria del Monte*. Having climbed to the last of the chapels you come across the *Pogliaghi* museum, which is crammed to overflowing with various art collections and the famous plaster-cast of the main doors of Milan Cathedral. (Open April to September, Tues.–Sun., 10 am–noon and 2.30–5.30 pm. Closed Mon.)

At the turn-off for *Campo dei Fiori* a road goes up to the gardens of the former Grand Hotel at a height of 1,033 m. From here it is just a few minutes' walk to the *Cima Tre Croci* which, being the best vantage point in Lombardy, is known as *il piu bel balcone*. In good weather the view extends over the lakes as far as the ice faces of the Monte Rosa mountains. Both Sacro Monte and Campo dei Fiori, incidentally, can be reached from Varese by bus.

A special tip
Connoisseurs of the good life exploring Sacro Monte should include in their itinerary a detour to the *Caffè Ristorante Borducan*. First take a look round the semicircular café furnished with old oak chairs and tables, and round the homely bar; then if the weather is fine step out on to the high balcony from where there is an incomparable view deep into Lombardy. Afterwards the proprietress will almost certainly offer you a glass of her home-made herb schnapps.

The gigantic Borromeo statue, Arona

The western shore
Arona Pop. 16,000
As you come from the south the first place of note on the west side of Lake Maggiore is Arona. Facing it on the opposite side of the lake is the Angera fortress, already referred to. Arona has established itself as a summer resort mainly for Italian holidaymakers but has also made a name for itself as a commercial town. Its urban origins are most probably owed to the Gauls, while later on it attained economic and strategic importance under the Saxon emperors. The long lakeside promenade, parts of which run beneath pergolas, provides a truly delightful walk.

Europe's biggest statue
Considerable effort is required in order to experience this 'Eighth Wonder of the World', but do climb up to the *Colosso di San Carlone*, a 21-m-high statue erected in 1697 in honour of St Charles Borromeo. Appointed archbishop of Milan at the early age of twenty-two, St

Charles is one of the patron saints of the Jesuit order.

Even when first cast the copper figure cost the enormous sum of 1,200,000 Milan lire, which goes a long way to explaining why this giant is still the largest statue in Europe. Everything about it is gargantuan: the head has a circumference of 6.5 m, the feet are as big as boats, and the copper folds of the cassock are like small valleys. A steep ladder allows you to climb up the inside of the great statue.

Stendhal was so impressed by the monument that in 1800 he wrote to his sister Pauline: 'This statue commands the lake in silence. Its peace was long undisturbed until a short while ago during the siege of Arona when a cannonball struck its breast, luckily without damaging it. Never have I seen a finer image.'

Lesa Pop. 2,500

A small rather sleepy village which still contrives to stand somewhat aloof from the hustle and bustle of tourism. From its tiny but very spick and span lakeside promenade you have a superb view of the opposite shore as far as Campo dei Fiori near Varese. Grand villas with equally grand gardens have spread themselves on its outskirts. The mild climate prevailing here ensures that the area abounds with excellent fruit.

Belgirate Pop. 600

Belgirate is a cheerful little place surrounded by villas and gardens, all capable of being taken in with a single glance. From the lakeside promenade the eye wanders naturally to Lake Maggiore's other shore, near Ispra. The elderly in particular can feel at ease in Belgirate. Stendhal also loved this tiny village, in which the narrow alleyways are still kept largely free of motor traffic.

 Directly behind the parish church you will catch sight of the ochre-coloured *Villa Cairoli*. It once belonged to Benedetto Cairoli, a politician of revolutionary bent who took part in the 1848 uprising in Milan and was later a member of Garibaldi's band of partisans.

Sailing school; watersports and sailing club.

Stresa Pop. 5,200

Though it is quite small Stresa's experience of tourism already extends over more than a hundred years. Kings and composers used to come here; the noble and wealthy from all over the world were once attracted to it. Today this congress centre and spa still abounds with magnificent buildings of the Belle Epoque, such as the *Regina Palace* hotel. Surrounded by gardens ablaze with colour they line the promenade, with its fine show of palms and roses. It is a fashionable and expensive resort which has recently become much livelier.

In fact Stresa is suffering something of a crisis of identity. Villa upon villa and garden upon garden, all of them gorgeous, proclaim wealth and prosperity on every corner. At the same time the city fathers of this affluent little place have bowed to the inevitable and made their concessions to mass tourism. So kitsch and commerce flourish in the quaint alleys. It is boom time for a highly profitable souvenir industry!

Lake Maggiore: the western shore

 A zoo in a superb setting

About 2 km south of the centre of town large signposts point the way to the zoo at the *Villa Pallavicino*. Here twisting woodland paths lead among tall stone-pines and chestnuts to a waterfall tumbling from rock to rock between ferns and spiraeas. Rare birds fill the aviaries, and all kinds of animals romp and frisk in the enormous enclosures. This splendid park covers an area of over 16 hectares. Since it descends right down to the waterside it also opens up a magnificent view over Lake Maggiore. Anyone with children should certainly set aside at least half a day for a visit. Spitting llamas, chattering monkeys, droll mountain goats, graceful flamingos, inquisitive pygmy parrots, sociable sea-lions — a motley bunch awaits you here!

The zoo is open daily (from mid-March until mid-November, 8.30 am—7 pm). The delightful Villa Pallavicino itself however is not open to the public. Built in the 19th c. in classical style it remains in the possession of the many-branched Pallavicino family.

 Very well-equipped marina.

  Sailing school and yacht club.

 Several open-air pools in Stresa.

 Monte Mottarone

There are three ways of getting up Monte Mottarone (1,491 m). You can walk up in four hours, drive up — almost to the summit — in a quarter of an hour, or be carried up by cable car. Whichever way you choose it is certainly well worth going! In good conditions you will find a glorious canvas unfolding before your eyes: the Gulf of Borromeo on Lake Maggiore, to the north the jagged white peaks of the Alps, and to the south-east the plain from which in clear weather Milan greets you from beneath its veil of haze. The summit of Mottarone is rightly considered one of the best vantage points in Europe.

If you decide to go by car don't miss two treats on the way back. Concealed within the walls of the health resort of *Gignese* (700 m) there is a real curiosity to be discovered, an umbrella and parasol museum founded in 1939. And at *Alpino*, which is a little higher up than Gignese, a famous alpine garden has been established. If you have the stamina you can examine some 2,000 varieties of mountain and medicinal plants.

The Borromean islands

Stresa is undoubtedly the most popular departure point for the Borromean islands. The ferry crossing takes only a few minutes. *Isola Bella* is familiar to many as the subject of a popular song. But Isola Bella is only one of three tiny islands. Close by is *Isola Madre*, its ochre-coloured palazzo disappearing beneath a cascade of exotic plants. The third is *Isola dei Pescatori*, of the three the one which has most kept its original character. It lies further offshore in the middle of the gulf, unexploited in its sylvan loveliness.

Ferries run to the islands from several lake resorts apart from Stresa. Ingenious use of the timetables allows you to combine visits to Isola Bella and Isola dei Pescatori, spending as long as you like on each. Isola Madre, however, has a service of its own and so has to be visited separately.

Lake Maggiore: the western shore

Borromeo Palace, Isola Bella

Isola Bella. During the summer months arrival on Isola Bella brings with it an initial shock in the form of bombardment with trashy souvenirs of every kind: ashtrays, shells, jewellery and postcards, often dear and usually tasteless. Then again there is the maelstrom of sightseers eager to visit the Borromeo Palace which was built between 1650 and 1671 and has since played host to many an emperor, king and artist, among them Richard Wagner. The palazzo is chock-a-block with works of art including paintings by Bramantino, Caravaggio, Tintoretto and Leonardo da Vinci. In addition there is an important collection of porcelain, a collection of arms, 16th c. Flemish tapestries, valuable antique furniture, mosaics, marblework, puppet theatres and musical instruments.

An external staircase leads from the palazzo's Gobelin gallery down into the park, whose ten terraces are laid out with plants of intoxicating colour and scent – camellias, acacias, lemon- and orange-trees, cedars of Lebanon, agaves, rubber-trees, Indian tamarisks and Chinese tea plants. The arrangement of the terraces is supposed to mirror that of the Hanging Gardens of Babylon. Completing the Baroque setting are stone figures, small pyramids, fountains, ponds and pergolas. (A guided tour – available in English – will add to your enjoyment of the gardens as well as of the palazzo.) Every handful of soil for the gardens was brought by Count Vitaliano from the mainland 300 years ago. What is so special about the gardens is that the lake and the mountains are in view from every corner. As to its name, legend has it that when the island was still no more than a piece of bare rock, one of the Borromeo counts thought it the perfect place to secrete a young lady called Isabella away from the prying eyes of a jealous wife.

Still intoxicated by the exuberant splendour of Isola Bella's Baroque you should straight away board the ferry for a taste of a wholly different draught on Isola dei Pescatori, 'fishermen's island'.

Isola dei Pescatori. The islanders here really do live by fishing. It is also a place of such overwhelming beauty that artists are its constant visitors. It is characterised by its narrow streets, fishermen's houses, two hotels, and its cheerful people content with just the wherewithal to live and who still clatter along the uneven alleyways in wooden-soled sandals. While on this tranquil island be sure to make the short trip to the parish church of *San Vittore* with its Baroque altars and impressive campanile.

Isola Madre. The great charm of Isola Madre, largest of the three islands, lies in its profusion of exotic plants. An enchanting elevated garden on five terraces scarcely leaves space for the 18th c. palazzo. A hundred-year-old wistaria, a palm tree a full metre in diameter, a giant Kashmir cypress and a massive cedar of Lebanon overshadowing the Borromeo Palace are only four exceptional examples of the island's many botanical delights. Coffee bushes and Chinese tea plants do so well in the subtropical climate that they are able to survive without any protection from the cold.

Like Isola Bella this island was also a favourite of many a crowned head, and writers such as Stendhal, Dickens, Dumas, Turgenev, Flaubert and Anatole France came to pay their respects. In their memoirs and their stories all have celebrated the Grande Dame of Lake Maggiore.

Baveno Pop. 4,500

Baveno knows plenty about tourism even if the town does stand somewhat in the shadow of neighbouring Stresa. In the last century Queen Victoria used to enjoy staying here. Fame and reputation came to it mainly on account of its mineral springs (believed to be effective in the treatment of metabolic disorders), but also because of the rose-coloured granite caves at the foot of Monte Mottarone.

If you take a steamer trip from here you will automatically come across a very special building, the lakeside *waiting room*. It stands resplendent in the purity of its Art Nouveau style, something of a rarity in Italy.

The splendid *Villa Fedora* used to belong to the composer Umberto Giordano.

Sailing club.

Lake Orta

Drive further north along the lakeside, then turn inland and continue via Gravellona Toce to the north end of Lake Orta. This lake is a holiday secret closely guarded by the Italians. It nestles idyllically among low, wooded hills, dominated to the north-east by Monte Mottarone. It is about 13 km long and 2 km wide and measures 143 m at its deepest point. For many decades Lake Orta lay dreamily apart from all the holiday bustle, but more and more concessions have recently been made to the demands of holidaymakers from all over Europe.

Orta San Giulio Pop. 1,200

Old palazzi, grand villas and a 16th c. arcaded town hall immediately catch the visitor's eye. The town hall, painted with coats of arms, is rather an amazing sight, being supported on two rows of columns. With its narrow streets, old buildings and church of *Santa Maria*

Picturesque arcade in Orta

Assunta this little place is truly picturesque and tranquil.

Pebble and gravel beach almost the whole of which shelves steeply down into the lake. Lake Orta is not the best place for bathing and is particularly unsuitable for children.

Sailing club.

The brisk wind which blows almost constantly over the lake makes this a paradise for windsurfing.

Around Orta there are several camping and caravan sites, all in lovely locations.

There is a riding school at *Miasino* 2 km inland. Rides organised across delightful, hilly countryside.

Ex Even out-of-practice walkers can easily reach the top of *Sacro Monte* (400 m) with its twenty pilgrim chapels dating from the 17th and 18th c. The climb begins from behind the parish church and takes about three-quarters of an hour. There is a vantage point among the stone-pines and beeches which offers a beautiful view of the west side of the lake.

Isola di San Giulio. It takes only a few minutes to be transported here by motorboat and into another world. The 4th c. *basilica* and 11th c. campanile stand amid beautifully laid out terraced gardens, the church interior being adorned with old frescos. The black marble pulpit dates from the 12th c. All are encircled within a protective girdle of houses overlooking the lake. The single restaurant is in an imposing villa in the centre of the island. You can enjoy a glass of wine sitting at the windows with a view out over the lake.

The west shore with its single tiny village of *Pella* is less well endowed. While it does not really warrant a stay, it is worth seeing this part of Lake Orta by devoting half a day to driving round the lake (38 km).

Verbania Pop. 32,000

Our route now takes us from timeless rural scenery past the little 2-km-long *Lago di Mergozzo* (with a couple of campsites on its shores for nature-loving holidaymakers), back to Lake Maggiore and into the elegance of Pallanza, which together with Intra forms the community known as Verbania. The location is fabulous: gorgeous gardens spread across the south-facing slopes of *Monte Rosso* to the sharply pointed headland with spectacular views of all three arms of Lake Maggiore.

Since this is a conference centre 'tranquil' is a word which fits it only to a limited extent. Occasionally some not very pleasant fumes waft over from the neighbouring industrial town of Intra and then it is time to make for the enclosed alleyways of the Old Town, many of which have splendidly ornate houses well worth seeing. Pallanza has some very presentable hotels and pensions to suit all pockets. Boating enthusiasts will find excellent facilities here. The *Museo del paesaggio* (landscape paintings) is in the *Palazzo Viani Dugnani* (open daily except Mon., 10 am–noon and 3–6 pm).

The botanical garden

The *Villa Taranto* just north of Verbania is a place of pilgrimage for plant-lovers the world over. The 20-hectare park was laid out in 1931 by a Scotsman, Captain Neil McEacharn. Many thousands of plant species imported from far and wide have slowly acclimatised to conditions here. These exotic beauties are watered directly from the lake by means of a sophisticated pumping system which makes it possible to supply every corner of the extensive grounds. Enter the domain of the lotus flower, and see if you can distinguish between 300 varieties of dahlias!

The magnificent gardens can be reached by bus from Verbania though ample car-parking space is also available. They are open from April 1st to October 31st, 8.30 am–6.30 pm. There are guides who will show you round for a fee, but unfortunately rather too few of them.

Rowing boats and small pedalos can be hired at the marina.

A local boatyard will do on-the-spot repairs if your motorboat happens to give trouble.

Sailing club; sailing school.

Several very good open-air swimming pools in the town centre.

Ferries leave throughout the day for nearly every resort on Lake Maggiore. Car ferries to Laveno.

Cannero Riviera Pop. 1,300

The climate here is especially mild so many holidaymakers come to the village during the winter months as well. Lemon- and orange-trees thrive in the open all the year round. Be sure you don't just drive through the streets of modern villas a little way up the hill but also walk down to the lakeside by way of the narrow alleyways. At the harbour colourful boats, rose-clad walls, palms and ochre-coloured houses blend together as if in a scene from a painting. Offshore are two picturesque ruined castles on rocky islets. The road which climbs steeply up from the jetty turns into a cascade during a sudden downpour. Then the dark granite tiles with which the houses are roofed gleam like the purest silver.

This is a place where anyone seeking peace and quiet will feel thoroughly at ease.

Hard courts belonging to the hotels.

Several campsites.

Cannobio Pop. 5,500

As so often on the lake, here too you must leave the main road taking you straight through the village in order to encounter *Old Cannobio*. The lakeside promenade is distinguished by its houses raised on low arches; their façades were once brightly painted but are now faded. Cannobio isn't smart, and the fashionable set never descends upon it. Instead it offers peace and quiet, a pleasant beach and good food. In the Middle Ages this fortified little place came into the possession of the Visconti, later (in 1441) passing to the Borromeo family. In 1859 the townsfolk fought courageously against an Austrian fleet which suddenly made its appearance on the lake.

A lovely beach which doesn't shelve too steeply into the lake, with fine gravel and generally clean water. Not overcrowded either.

Sailing school.

Hard courts belonging to the hotels.

A number of clean, well-tended sites around the village.

To *Carmine Superiore*, 3 km south, an old village with grey stone houses and a view of the lake.

Brissago Pop. 2,200

Driving into Brissago by the main road, to be confronted first by functional but characterless modern building, you may be excused disappointment. And yet you have actually arrived in quite a popular bathing resort which, in the 19th c., was already playing host to many an illustrious guest. In 1897, for example, Ruggiero Leoncavallo worked here on his opera *La Bohème* (not to be confused with Puccini's opera of the same name). The atmosphere of Brissago was sufficient to inspire him to write what, apart from his *Bajazzo*, turned out to be his best work.

Although this is actually Swiss territory the architecture of the town centre is still pure Italian.

Well-tended campsite.

Regular ferry services to Brissago's two little islets.

Ascona Pop. 4,500

Unless you are the fortunate owner of a property here (as indeed are many foreigners who appreciate the security and tax advantages offered by Switzerland), you will probably just be paying a brief visit to this beautifully manicured pleasure ground of millionaires and multimillionaires. It wouldn't occur to a normal mortal with an average bank balance to stay here for any length of time, the price of food and accommodation being simply too steep. But anyway, as mentioned already, Ascona is a place of summer residence rather than a holiday resort.

A little town where writers like Erich Maria Remarque and Hans Habe, who were also connoisseurs of good living, chose to make their home can naturally be expected to have its charms. Among them are the road along the lake with its magnificent plantains and the *piazza*, Ascona's 'salon' where especially in the afternoons a colourful cosmopolitan crowd gathers to enjoy a relaxed chat.

Right next to the church in Ascona is the *Casa Serodine*, also known as the *Casa Borrani*. This superb house was once the home of the Serodini, the famous family of painters and sculptors who worked in Austria as well as here in the Tessin. Decorated with splendid frescos it is now a second-hand bookshop.

Sailing school, frequently fully booked way in advance.

Locarno Pop. 15,000

Locarno is often mentioned in the same breath as Ascona. Similarly awash with wealth and prosperity the locality has a favourable climate and exceptionally enchanting scenery. Holiday homes have consequently sprouted everywhere and climb high up the wooded slopes.

Locarno is certainly no longer the chic spa it once was. Those days are over and it has become noisy and busy with something of a big-city atmosphere. Long, wide, perfectly straight roads cross the town. Even so, if you are not in a hurry and can spend a few days here you will soon fall in love with it. Its attraction lies in the Old Town with its narrow streets where you can try all

Ascona harbour, Lake Maggiore

manner of speciality sausages in a homely Swiss restaurant called the *Tessiner Teller* — though there are also plenty of equally homely osterias in keeping with the still very Italian character of the place. The long lakeside promenade with its magnificent show of plants is a real joy to behold.

Sailing school.

Several very good open-air pools in the town.

Ex Locarno-Monti

You should some time make an excursion by way of Muralto to Locarno-Monti, the adopted home of Europe's intellectual élite and wealthy aristocracy. Superb villas are set among the trees on the wooded hillside and the view of the lake is stunning. People in the film industry, too — scriptwriters, directors, actors and producers — seem to have made this little spot their own. Many a bright idea for a film has been dreamed up here.

There is a very pleasant walk which goes along the narrow Via al Sasso and up to various superb vantage points. Stop and take a rest at the Hotel Belvedere, an impressive 17th c. palazzo where you can enjoy a well-earned coffee in a room with a colossal chimneypiece and full of lavish paintings. The object of the excursion is to visit the 17th c. pilgrim church of *Madonna del Sasso* which is well worth seeing. The interior contains lovely stucco decorations, and a pietà by Stella (1547) on the high altar.

Nearly every resort on Lake Maggiore can be reached by steamer or hydrofoil from Locarno, with departures virtually every hour. Round trips are also possible.

The Locarno Pact

The aim of the pact, worked out at the Locarno Conference (October 5th to 16th 1925), was to enable the German Empire to rejoin the community of European powers following the First World War. The signatories were Belgium, Germany, France, Great Britain, Italy, Poland and Czechoslovakia.

The pact, signed in Locarno on October 16th and ratified in London on December 1st 1925, consisted of a series of agreements on security, the Rhineland and Germany's western frontier. The main treaty was one of mutual guarantee between the signatories. It pronounced inviolable Germany's western frontier as established by the Treaty of Versailles, and provided for the Rhineland to be maintained as a demilitarised zone. It further included a non-aggression pact and an agreement among the parties to settle all differences peacefully. Great Britain and Italy undertook to uphold the terms of the treaty by coming to the defence of any signatory threatened by its violation. The German foreign minister Gustav Stresemann refused any guarantee of Germany's eastern frontier.

The main treaty was supplemented by individual arbitration agreements between Germany and Belgium, France, Poland and Czechoslovakia. As a result of the treaties Germany was admitted to the League of Nations and a period of détente ensued.

During the course of the negotiations it became clear time and again that both the mistrust of Germany by its former adversaries and the German Empire's mistrust of the politics of the League were still very far from being overcome. While the terms were being negotiated in Locarno, nationalists, mainly German and French, repeatedly tried to obstruct their statesmen's policy of reconciliation. The delegations spent days and nights in heated discussion. It was aboard a steamer on Lake Maggiore that the German chancellor Luther, foreign minister Stresemann and his British and French colleagues Chamberlain and Briand finally achieved the long-awaited agreement.

In 1926 Aristide Briand and Gustav Stresemann received the Nobel Peace Prize for their part in concluding the Locarno Pact. Sir Joseph Austen Chamberlain, who had mediated between Germany and France during the difficult negotiations in Locarno, had already been honoured with the Nobel Prize the year before.

As a result of Hitler's armament policy and the entry of German troops into the Rhineland, the Treaty of Locarno was revoked on March 3rd 1936.

Right: Tremezzo – on Lake Como's 'Azalea Riviera'

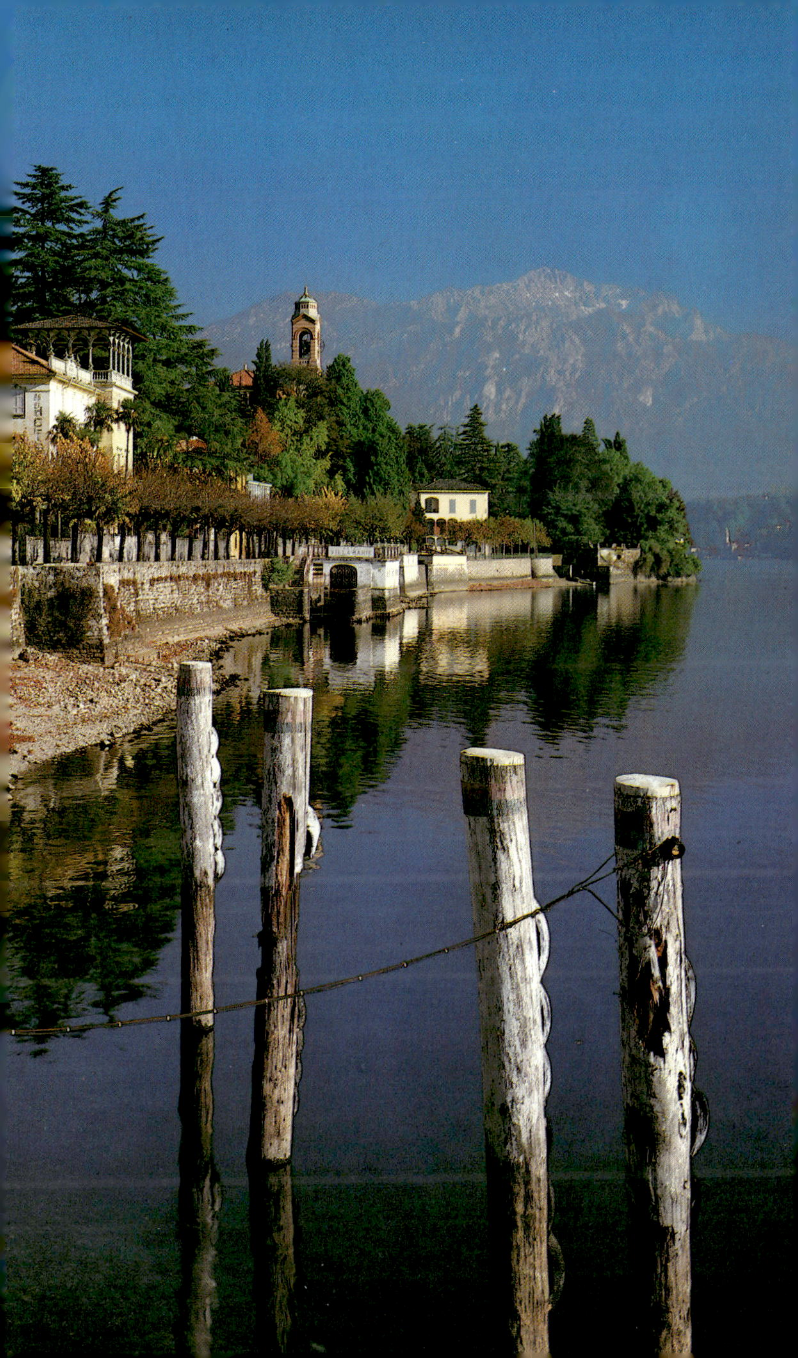

Lake Como

Among the many superlatives applied to it there is one that isn't likely to be experienced at first hand: at 410 m Lake Como is the deepest inland water in Europe! 50 km long and about 4.5 km wide for most of its length, it is framed by mountains which rise to heights of 2,000 m, and lies wreathed in olive- and fig-trees, cypresses, and villa gardens with a breathtaking luxuriance of flowers. Many people regard it as the most beautiful lake in the world. Although with a surface area of 146 sq km it is only the third largest lake in northern Italy, because of its shape — an inverted Y — it has the longest shoreline.

The Romans arrived here in the 2nd c. BC, their patricians idling away their time in the first luxury villas to be built on the lake. But for the new rulers the pleasures of the place were soon to be tempered by increasing danger. The barbarians threatened from the north and for the Romans Lake Como suddenly assumed strategic importance. A military road, the Via Regia, starting in Milan and continuing into Gallic Rhaetia, was constructed along its western shore.

Lake Como is a holiday area capable of satisfying many tastes. The most beautiful part is unquestionably the central section, where the three arms of the lake meet. Some visitors are interested only in the simple things, the lake itself, the slate-roofed houses lining the narrow streets, and the gardens ablaze with flowers. Others arrive already well read and laden with cultural baggage. They want to feel themselves following in the footsteps of famous people, the poets, dictators, statesmen, writers and musicians who have all spent time here, from the Emperor Barbarossa to Napoleon and Queen Victoria . . . and the likes of Flaubert, Foscolo, Bellini and Liszt who have rather more intellectual appeal. Images of André Gide's libertine forays on the lake, and of Kafka's fleeting stay, float into the mind, as too does the memory of Mussolini's inglorious execution in Mezzegra after he had been taken prisoner at Dongo while fleeing to Switzerland. Churchill was another to spend time here, not for political reasons but in search of artistic inspiration.

Lake Como also has to cope of course with the mass tourist who, in the haste of a lightning visit, confuses Isola Comacina, its only island, with Isola Bella. And the lake is the talk of the international jet set as well, drawn mainly to its close-woven and attractive network of luxury hotels. Just to contemplate these mansions, which the travel guides describe with words like princely, fills the observant visitor with admiration for the architecture of the buildings, but produces mixed feelings about the people who commissioned them. What after all was life like a hundred years ago? Sweet beyond compare for the fortunate few who lived in these palaces, but a lowly and arduous existence for the host of peasants, craftsmen and servants — including some very educated men employed as tutors by distinguished families like the Serbelloni and the Porro.

Walking through the more than ample grounds of one of these villas it is easy enough to visualise how those most privileged of people spent their days. In front of the grand house the garden, lakeside landing stage and terraces are set in parkland landscaped in the English fashion but full of exotic plants and tropical flowers planted with scrupulous precision and regardless of cost. (In one corner are the peasants' humble homes, built directly against the stables.) The owner's family and guests would stay here mainly in the autumn, because in those days sunbathing and a tanned skin were far from being fashionable. They whiled away their time with sumptuous meals and extravagant parties, engaging musicians and *literati* to divert them. This was the time of year when the rich spent their idleness most pleasurably, in sporting activities and games, *affaires de coeur*, tittle-tattle, and picnics in the country.

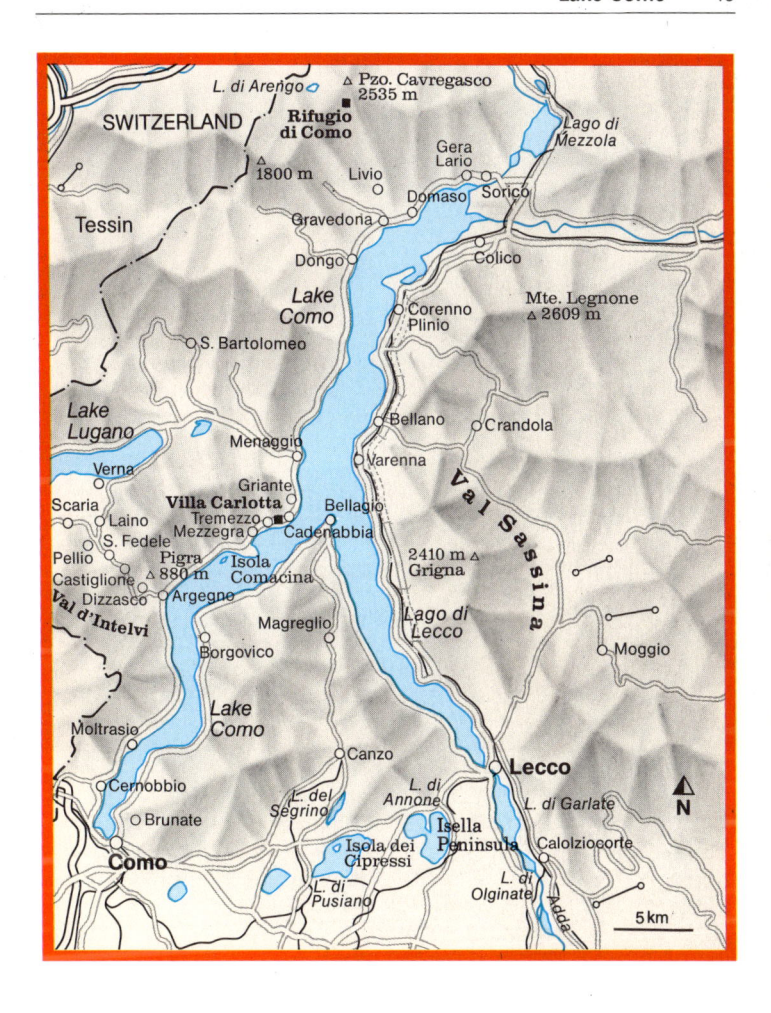

With the decline in the fortunes of the great families, some of these villas became luxury hotels. Since then they have been open to a less grand but still far from deprived section of society.

The gardens of the Villa Melzi, Bellagio, Lake Como

The western shore
Como Pop. 95,000

Situated at the extreme south-west end of the lake is the city which gives it its name. Anyone who wants a comprehensive view of Como should immediately climb into the cable car and go up to *Brunate* (716 m).

Como manages successfully to be both an industrial city and a holiday resort. It is known as the 'silk town', the excellent fabrics manufactured by local textile factories being exported all over the world.

The layout of the Old Town goes back to Roman times when it was the site of an important military camp. Both Pliny the Elder and Pliny the Younger were born here.

Relics from all ages

Strongly recommended is a visit to the *Museo Civico*, the city museum (open 9.30 am–noon and 2–5 pm, Sun. 9.15 am–noon; closed Mon.). It houses a truly impressive collection of prehistoric and Roman relics, as well as items from the Middle Ages.

Although it is nearly 600 years old, parts of Como's *cathedral* can almost be said to be new! It was built in 1396 at the bidding of the Visconti, replacing the older 11th c. church of S. Maria Maggiore, but some 350 years went by before its completion with the construction of the dome. It is generally considered one of the outstanding examples of Renaissance architecture in Lombardy. Standing in the *Piazza del Duomo* you can clearly see that the building is in two sections: the very spacious 15th c. Late Gothic nave, and the eastern end, the latter having been constructed over a lengthy period from the 16th to the 18th c. Among the many superb items which embellish the interior, two works of art are especially worth seeing, an altarpiece by Leonardo's pupil Bernardo Luini (1490–1532) and *The Marriage of the Virgin* by the Piedmontese-Lombard artist Gaudenzio Ferrari (1470–1546).

Wandering through the Old Town you will notice many houses with stone, stucco and wrought-iron ornamentation. The wrought-iron work dates mainly from the 18th and 19th c.

Do not miss the church of *Sant' Agostino*, founded by hermit monks in the 14th c. but completely rebuilt in 1773. In the interior are four wonderful tapestries by Morazzone depicting scenes from the life of the Virgin.

Especially around the village of *Borgovico* and beyond, many lovely villas grace the lake shore, which runs northwards both east and west of Como. The most famous of all the country houses near Como is the neoclassical *Villa Olmo*. It is supposed to have got its name from a gigantic elm which according to legend was planted by Pliny the Younger. Today the palazzo is owned by the city authorities and is used for numerous cultural events. Its columned façade overlooks the lake while in the equally beautiful interior the stucco work, gilding, statuary and frescos all catch the eye.

The water in the bay at Como is so polluted that in most places bathing is banned. In compensation there are a number of public swimming pools.

Yacht club.

Cernobbio Pop. 7,700

This trim little place close to the Swiss border has, like Como, achieved an excellent resolution of the conflict between industry (silk- and papermills) and tourism. A visitor's first impressions

Cable car at Como

Villa d'Este gardens

are all pleasing – well-kept hotels, villas and gardens clothing the hillside, and the Italian garden in the village itself. Of the many villas the palatial 16th c. *Villa d'Este* most deserves a mention. Altered at the beginning of the 19th c. (and now a luxury hotel), it was the home of Caroline of Brunswick, hapless wife of the future George IV. The splendid garden is ornamented with grottos, ponds and cascades.

Hotel bathing enclosure, blessed with a divine backdrop.

Moltrasio Pop. 2,100

Some of the buildings which make up this delightful little spot follow the curving shoreline, others perch high on the slopes above. This is one of the less well-known resorts. Its special attraction lies in the enchanting view of the lake.

Ex To *Monte Bisbino* (1,329 m), 13 km away.

Argegno Pop. 700

A rather modest, quiet little place, though fully geared to tourism. Its main claim to distinction lies in its position at one end of the Val d'Intelvi. From here both the valley and Lake Lugano are within easy reach.

9-hole course in Lanzo d'Intelvi.

Ex Pigra, Val d'Intelvi and Isola Comacina

There is a glorious vista over the lake from the top of *Pigra* (880 m; a cable car runs from the centre of Argegno).

You should also have a car available to enable you to spend a day in the *Val d'Intelvi*. It is surprising that the Val d'Intelvi is still generally so little known, because for hundreds of years this 'valley of artists' spread inspiration across Europe, especially during the Baroque period. Leave Argegno by the winding, narrow but otherwise good mountain road to Muronico and Dizzasco. The first of the larger villages is *Castiglione*, with its welcoming church of *Santo Stefano*. Then follow the road through S. Fedele to *Laino*. This remote village was the birthplace of Lorenzo degli Spazzi, architect of Milan and Como cathedrals. Next continue through Lanzo to the *Sighignola* viewpoint (1,300 m). From this somewhat exposed vantage point you should, with any luck, have a view over the whole of Lake Lugano.

From *Sala Comacina* you can take a boat to the *Isola Comacina*, which is the only island in Lake Como and is only 600 m long. It has a fish restaurant, the *Locanda dell'Isola*, which is open from March to October. At the end of June a procession with fireworks takes place on the island.

Val d'Intelvi – famous the world over

Lombardy has attracted many an artist, but it has also produced them, enriching the great centres of Italian art and transporting their genius to countries north of the Alps. Most famous of all are the master builders and stonemasons from around Lake Como, the *maestri comacini*, whose reputation was already established in the time of the Lombard kings. Until the 18th c. they were Lombardy's primary export commodity, their exceptional talents held in high esteem the length and breadth of Europe. They worked in Austria and Germany, Sweden and France.

Among the masons of Lake Como the men from a small and still relatively unknown valley, the Val d'Intelvi, were especially gifted. The full story of these master builders is still the subject of research, but even the studies so far available reveal that the number and importance of the buildings they constructed throughout Europe have been hugely underestimated.

In the 16th c. Lucio di Spazzi, born in the Val d'Intelvi, rebuilt Schloss Hohenschangau near Füssen for the Augsburg aristocrat Johann Baumgartner. The men from the valley cultivated their craftsmen's skills over generations, passing them on from father to son. Following no predetermined routes they journeyed to Serbia and into the Pyrenees, to Neuchâtel and Liège, Catalonia and Aquitaine. They saw a great deal on their travels, and they worked hard, some as master builders, some *sine magistro* as simple masons. What they found to admire in an alien culture they adopted, to be brought home and refined.

Several of the *maestri intelvesi* founded schools in distant places, the Gagini for instance in Sicily. The achievements of these master builders, stone-carvers and masons, fresco-painters, and artists in stucco work and plaster extended over eleven centuries, from the 7th c. to the 18th.

Almost every village in the Val d'Intelvi has something to show of the expertise of its craftsmen. There is a superb Romanesque doorway for example in the church of *S. Fedele*, and in *Cerano* a Romanesque campanile.

The most famous artist families of the area are the Carloni from Scaria, the Solari from Verna and the Bregno from Osteno.

Tremezzo Pop. 1,500

If you are already enthusing about Lake Como, prepare now to have your breath taken away. Nowhere is the lake shown to better advantage than here at Tremezzo where its full glory is revealed. Not for nothing is the *Riviera Tremezzina* also called the *Azalea Riviera*, and ever since the Middle Ages it has been known as the land of eternal spring.

This is where the lake turns to run in a more northerly direction, bringing the 3,000-m-high snow-clad mountains of Switzerland into open view. Although you could be forgiven for thinking that the whole village must be populated entirely with north Italians, who own the lovely houses here, in fact there are always hotels and pensions enough for passing visitors. Tremezzo is a tourist resort from top to bottom and it is hard to know what to mention first, the outstanding restaurants or the excellent sport and leisure facilities.

Tremezzo also has the merit that you can jump confidently into the lake for a refreshing bathe, but don't expect a beach, not even a pebbly one. To get to the water you must first cross the road and then usually go down a few stone steps directly into the cool water. Not for children therefore! Comfortably large swimming pools are found in many of the hotels, however, even the middle-category ones.

First-class Italian fare at reasonable prices in the *Balognett* pizzeria bar and the *Al Veluu* restaurant.

Villa Carlotta

Between Tremezzo and Cadenabbia is one of the great attractions on Lake Como, the *Villa Carlotta* (open from March to October, 9–11.30 am and 2–4.30 pm). The palace was built by the margrave Giorgio Clerici at the beginning of the 18th c., when the gardens were also laid out. Most of the interior furnishings however are courtesy of Count Sommariva who owned the villa from 1795 to 1856. The house later passed into the possession of Princess Marianne, wife of Adalbert of Prussia, and she bequeathed it to her daughter Charlotte whose name it has borne ever since.

Outside the villa a gorgeous panoply of flaming azalea blooms, rubber-trees, cedars of Lebanon, and ferns and orchids of all kinds welcomes the visitor, the azaleas and rhododendrons being particularly dazzling in April and May.

Cadenabbia/Griante Pop. 900

A wide but busy tree-lined avenue connects Tremezzo with Cadenabbia which 150 years ago consisted of only a few fishermen's and boatmen's houses. Today it is a thriving holiday resort chock-a-block with villas and hotels. Even so, such is the luxuriance of the vegetation in between them on the slopes that the little township absorbs its bevy of tourists with no hint of a bursting seam. Cadenabbia is actually just the lakeside part of Griante, a residential district on the hillside beyond. Numerous cafés and bars have opened in the main street, intruding at frequent intervals into the long line of majestic hotels.

Villa La Collina

In 1977 the Konrad Adenauer Foundation acquired the Villa La Collina which Konrad Adenauer at one time called his second home. Until 1966 the first ever chancellor of the Federal Republic of Germany used to spend his holidays in

Cadenabbia. Here he wrote his memoirs, and received many distinguished visitors. Here too the famous portraits by Graham Sutherland and Oskar Kokoschka were painted, and photographs of the *boccia*-playing chancellor were taken. From the villa's terraces and balconies there are fine views of the gardens, the lake and the Alps. La Collina is unfortunately not open to the public at fixed times, only by prior arrangement with the caretaker.

Although you can bathe in the lake itself many of the Milanese who spend the summer here still prefer to go to the 'Lido', the well-kept but expensive swimming pool on a terrace above the lake. The pool has a restaurant with good service and affordable prices.

Good food, particularly fish, at the *Albergo Ristorante Rodrigo* in the main street, and at *Marianna*, 57 Via Regina.

Hourly to Bellagio and Varenna.

Menaggio Pop. 3,000

Menaggio is situated on a small promontory only 4 km north of Cadenabbia and enjoys a reputation for excellent accommodation and sports facilities. The piazza, which is open to the lake, is given added character by romantic pergolas and a two-storeyed arcaded house. Churchill visited Menaggio and captured the beauty of this little place in a number of paintings.

Public swimming pool. Pools in the larger hotels.

18-hole course at Grandola 3.7 km away.

Hourly to Bellagio and Varenna.

Gravedona Pop. 2,700

Menaggio and Gravedona are worlds apart. Gravedona is a delightful old lakeside parish, still scarcely touched by tourism. From the church of *Santa Maria delle Grazie* you get a fine panorama over the village. Gravedona's past is rich in history as its palazzi and old churches (like the 12th c. *Santa Maria del Tiglio*) testify.

Sailing club.

Hill walks to the *Rifugio di Como* (1,800 m) and *Lago di Arengo*, an idyllic mountain lake beyond.

Ex Around the northern half of the lake the lure of the mountains is irresistible. Livio, at 660 m, is a good base for climbing enthusiasts and can be reached by car from Gravedona. It is also the starting point for relatively easy expeditions on foot to *Pizzo Cavregasco* and *Pizzo Ledù* (both about 2,500 m).

Lago di Mezzola

By driving north through Domaso, Gera Lario and Sorico and then crossing the River Mera you come to Lago di Mezzola, the headwaters of Lake Como hundreds of years ago, before two separate lakes were formed. Today it is about 3 km long and 2 km wide. Except for an abundance of fish which makes it popular with anglers the lake cannot really be said to have any special charm. Not to be regarded as essential sightseeing.

From Novate, to Codera.

The eastern shore
Colico Pop. 6,000

At Colico too the attractions of the area stem less from the lake than from the mountains. It lies surrounded by magnificent mountain scenery with the peaks of Chiavenna to the north and the massive Monte Legnone (2,609 m) to the east. In the 17th c. this little village was devastated by numerous wars.

Sailing club and sailing school.

Ideal base for hill-walking and for mountaineering expeditions, with or without a guide.

6 km from Colico is the abbey of *Piona*. Inside the restored 11th c. monastery church there are remnants of Byzantine frescos. Also highly recommended is the pleasant drive to the peaceful valleys of the Valtellina.

A special tip

Half-way between Colico and Bellano you'll come across *Corenno Plinio*, a small village which remains more permeated by the Middle Ages than anywhere else on the lake. Make the slow climb up to the ruins of the enormous 14th c. castle, its massive and roughly built outer wall dominating the whole of the lakefront. Pick a clear day so that you can delight in the views of the lake and the mountains. If you're one of those people who don't always have to be restlessly ticking off one place after another, you'll feel in your element here.

Bellano Pop. 4,000

Now the second biggest community on the eastern shore of the lake, Bellano has resounded many times to the clash of arms. It was here that swords were crossed in the war between Como and Milan. Its people make their living mainly from the cotton industry, as artisans, and of course from tourism. The hotels, pensions and restaurants are good, and reasonable with it.

Bellano is anyway worth a visit if only to see the church of *Santi Nazaro e Celso*, a 14th c. building notable for its black and white façade in Lombardy's distinctive Gothic style.

Going east from the church turn off and follow the road uphill. After about ten minutes you reach a massive gorge called *Orrido*, which reverberates to the roar of the Pioverna's wildly foaming waters.

Sailing club in Bellano.

Bellano is a good starting point for an untaxing drive through the *Val Sassina*. Here the numerous little holiday resorts are popular with the Italians for winter sports. Some 3 km inland from Bellano there is also *Lezzeno* with an 18th c. pilgrim church.

Varenna Pop. 800

This tiny and extremely romantic little place basks in the glory of its unique location – it is here that the lake splits into its east and west branches. The scenery is majestic. In the middle the headland of Bellagio soars high to divide the lake, while Cadenabbia and Menaggio catch the eye on the opposite shore. The old part of Varenna is criss-crossed by a profusion of alleyways, almost all of them straight and descending steeply to the lake. Colour-washed house fronts, similar to those in some villages on the

Villa Monastero, Varenna

Ligurian coast, overlook the lake. Mainly in the upper part of the village the wealthy have built magnificent villas set in lush sub-tropical gardens.

The grounds of the *Villa Monastero* are open to the public daily from 10 am–6 pm. The Italian garden is particularly lovely, especially in May when the roses are in bloom. The villa itself, built in the 16th c. on the site of a convent, is now a scientific and cultural centre and closed to view.

Sailing club.

Lecco Pop. 51,000

There is nothing really to stop for between Varenna and Lecco — only industrial estates and modern housing — and at first Lecco itself takes some getting used to. The town, founded by the Romans, seems to be hemmed in on all sides by precipitous mountain walls. So even though Lecco lies at the southern end of Lake Como the town may appeal more to people who love mountains than to those of an aquatic bent.

The industriousness of Lecco's inhabitants is proverbial. In the Middle Ages they began breeding silkworms; a hundred years ago the iron and non-ferrous metal industries were born.

You will probably just pay a visit to Lecco; it is not likely to be chosen for an extended stay.

Above the town are the remains of the old 14th c. defences. Also of interest are the *cathedral* and the *Palazzo del Caleotto* where the novelist Alessandro Manzoni lived.

The Panorama swimming pool at the *Canottieri di Lecco* rowing club is recommended.

Sailing club.

Rowing and sailing boats for hire, also motorboats if you hold a driving licence. The best hire facilities are at the beach at *Canottieri di Lecco*.

Ex Small lakes off the beaten track

On the southern side of Lecco the River Adda makes a faint-hearted attempt to transform itself into two lakes, *Lago di Garlate* and *Lago di Olginate*, both named after the largest of the communities on their shores. These lakes are mentioned only to be forgotten, however; through no fault of their own they lie under a pall of industrial fumes from Lecco.

The air is cleaner if you turn west towards *Lago di Annone* and *Lago di Pusiano*. Jutting far out into Lago di Annone is the picturesque *Isella* peninsula; on it is an exceptionally pretty campsite with a superb view of the lake and the opposite shore. Lago di Pusiano

Panorama of Lake Como

also has its jewel, the *Isola dei Cipressi*, a small islet densely covered with dark cypresses.

From here the road leads past *Lago del Segrino*, a small and somewhat featureless expanse of water, to *Canzo* and *Magreglio*. Standing a few kilometres back from the shores of Lake Como, these are mentioned mainly because of the excellent riding opportunities for beginners and more experienced riders. There is also a popular walk to the *Corni di Canzo* (1,373 m).

Bellagio Pop. 3,200

Bellagio's unequalled position is matched by its outstanding reputation as a resort. Indeed for many people Bellagio is the pearl of Lake Como, a spa and holiday resort worthy of a place among the best in the world. Set off to perfection by glorious gardens, it is sited exactly at the fork of the inverted Y, on the furthest tip of the peninsula which divides the lake into its two branches, Como and Lecco.

Nowhere else on the lake enjoys a more strategically commanding position than Bellagio, so the Gauls constructed elaborate defence-works here. Pliny the Younger built his *Villa Tragoedia* on a hill above the town. The famous seem always to have been attracted to it, and Bellagio has played host to the Emperor Maximilian I, to Napoleon and to King Leopold I of Belgium.

The Roman poet Virgil sang its praises long ago, and artists visiting it since have included Leonardo da Vinci, Stendhal and Mark Twain. Franz Liszt and Marie d'Agoult lived here together and it was here that their daughter Cosima, Richard Wagner's future wife, was born.

Despite its thriving tourist trade the spa still contrives to be much the same as it was in the past. Worn steps, narrow streets and low arcades, exotic plants and magnificent gardens all remain unchanged.

Villa Serbelloni: now the property of an American foundation. Its 19th c. Italian gardens provide a breathtaking view embracing the two arms of the lake (two guided tours daily).

Villa Melzi: built in 1808 for Duke Francesco Melzi d'Eril, chief statesman of the Cisalpine Republic under Napoleon I. In the gardens the azaleas and rhododendrons particularly catch the eye. (Open daily from March to October, 9 am–12.30 pm and 2.30–6 pm, in summer 9 am–6.30 pm, no lunchtime closure.)

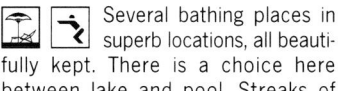

Several bathing places in superb locations, all beautifully kept. There is a choice here between lake and pool. Streaks of motorboat fuel in the lake usually make the pool advisable.

Regular open-air orchestral concerts.

There are steamer trips round the lake, as well as trips direct to almost any of the other lake resorts. Car ferries leave hourly for Varenna, Cadenabbia and Menaggio, and hydrofoils operate to the main resorts.

If you first take the boat to Varenna a two-and-a-half-hour walk will bring you to *Piano Rancio*, a viewpoint famous for its extensive carpet of narcissi.

A lovely five-and-a-half-hour climb in the mountains will get you to the top of *Grigna* (2,410 m). From the summit on a clear day there is a view all the way from the Matterhorn to the Ortler. Again you must first cross the lake to Varenna on the other shore.

Mountains framing Lake Lugano

Lake Lugano

Lake Lugano is a real mixture of the Italian and the Swiss. Put purely numerically 60 km of the shoreline belongs to Switzerland and about 34 km to Italy. Although now fragmented by the curious border which carves out three separate areas of Italian territory, the whole lake belongs historically to the ancient region of Lombardy. The shape of the lake is as strange as its frontier. While all the other lakes in northern Italy have a distinct north-south orientation, Lake Lugano is bizarrely convoluted, as well as being surrounded on all sides by steeply rising mountains. Being narrow for almost its entire length most of it lies in the shadow of peaks 2,000 to 3,000 m high. It is barely 50 sq km altogether, of which 32 sq km belongs to the Tessin – i.e. to Switzerland – and 18 sq km to Italy. That the lake lacks the attractive blue colour of its neighbours to east and west is primarily due to the large quantities of algae which float in it in summer making the water a murky green.

Nor can the great scenic charms of the lake hide the fact that in many places the water is polluted. Even today few of the lakeside communities are provided with adequate sewage treatment plants, and this is despite the fact that in most cases there is certainly no shortage of cash (not least because of the presence of the many foreigners owning second homes!). As well as the sewage which continues to flow freely into the lake there are also the many motorboats adding to the mix. Sometimes when the wind is unfavourable thick patches of yellow, green and violet oil shimmer on the water.

Hopefully the powers that be will soon wake up to the problem because, despite everything, the lake is still not beyond saving. And it must surely be saved, for the beauty of its scenery is in every respect the equal of Lakes Maggiore and Como.

Lake Lugano 57

Lugano Pop. 28,000

Lugano prospers on the wealth brought in by its leisured millionaires and congenial climate. With its very Swiss feel, it is often hard to credit that this was once part of Lombardy.

The city boasts two fine mountains which soar up from beside the water like towers: Monte San Salvatore to the south, 912 m high, and to the north-east Monte Brè which, though only 13 m higher, is much better known. It is dotted with luxury hotels and the villas of the super-rich.

Lugano has a lovely lakeside promenade of which it is rightly proud. It may be a bustling, enterprising, self-consciously commercial town, and it may be the stamping ground of pleasure-loving young people from rich homes who zoom around in their sports cars, but Lugano is still a place of venerable churches and palaces, of secluded villas from the Belle Epoque and of palm trees and magnolias in extensive parks. Anyone who takes the trouble to seek out the treasures hidden amongst its blocks and shopping arcades will be rewarded with many a pleasant surprise.

Be sure to visit the gallery at Baron Thyssen's *Villa Favorita* in Lugano-Castagnola, at the foot of Monte Brè. Special exhibitions are held there from Easter to October and are open daily except Mondays.

Until recently as many as 190 of the greatest names in the world of art could be found represented there. The Thyssen-Bornemisza collection was started in the 1920s and is now one of the richest private collections in the world. Because the Swiss authorities showed no interest in extending the Villa Favorita the Prado in Madrid has been the collection's permanent home since 1988.

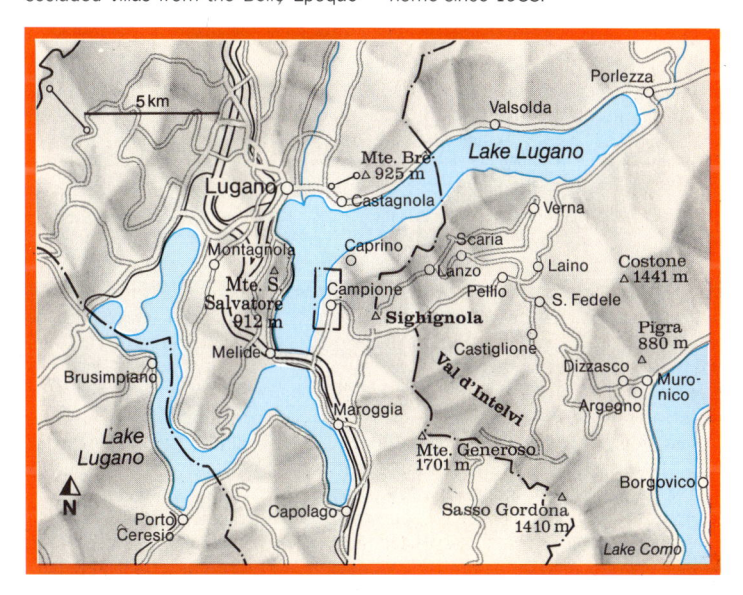

A number of very nice swimming pools in the town, most of them near the lake.

Sailing school.

Rowing boats and pedalos for hire.

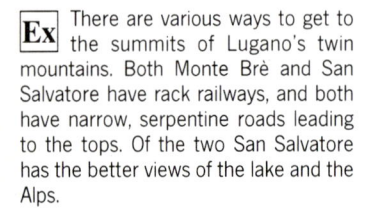

Ex There are various ways to get to the summits of Lugano's twin mountains. Both Monte Brè and San Salvatore have rack railways, and both have narrow, serpentine roads leading to the tops. Of the two San Salvatore has the better views of the lake and the Alps.

Montagnola Pop. 23,000

Drive south-west from Lugano and you are soon at Montagnola, another holiday playground for the world's wealthy, appreciative of the security offered by Switzerland. From here there is a lovely, commanding vista of the northernmost arm of Lake Lugano, still in view in its entirety. Stately villas hide behind high walls, and luxuriant vegetation is all around. The German writer Hermann Hesse lived in Montagnola from 1919 until his death in 1962. At first he lived in the *Casa Camuzzi* where for twelve years he had a flat. In 1931 he decided to buy a house, in which he spent the rest of his life. He once said of winter in the Tessin: 'I find it more beautiful than summer; it usually distinguishes itself with weeks of lovely weather.'

Campione Pop. 2,200

Diagonally across the lake from Lugano is Campione, an Italian enclave. In the Middle Ages this village produced generations of remarkable stonemasons who – like the craftsmen from

Campione, Lake Lugano

Lake Lugano

the Val d'Intelvi on Lake Maggiore – wandered throughout Europe from cathedral to cathedral and palazzo to palazzo. Today it is Campione's casino which enjoys a similarly widespread reputation amongst the *cognoscenti*. It is credited with the highest turnover at the roulette table in Europe. It is little wonder that so many film stars and *nouveaux riches* have moved into this customs paradise which levies no taxes, only water rates.

Campione's hotels and apartment blocks are new, clean and up to date; indeed except for one or two older villas looking a bit out of place everything about Campione is new, clean and up to date. The lakeside promenade from where you can look over to Lugano is dignified and attractive.

The former parish church of *S. Zenone* now houses collections of paintings and sculpture from the 14th and 15th c. The interior of *S. Maria dei Ghirli* is decorated with frescos by Lombard masters.

Several.

Sailing school.

In Lanzo d'Intelvi.

Try the *Crotti*. These lakefront wine cellars represent good value and can be highly recommended if you fancy mixing with a lively holiday crowd in a friendly and good-humoured atmosphere.

Ex Regular sailings mean that many of the resorts on Lake Lugano can be reached by steamer, including Lugano, Castagnola, Caprino, Melide, Maroggia and Capolago. Since you may find the timetable altered at short notice it is advisable whenever possible to check departure times the day before your planned excursion.

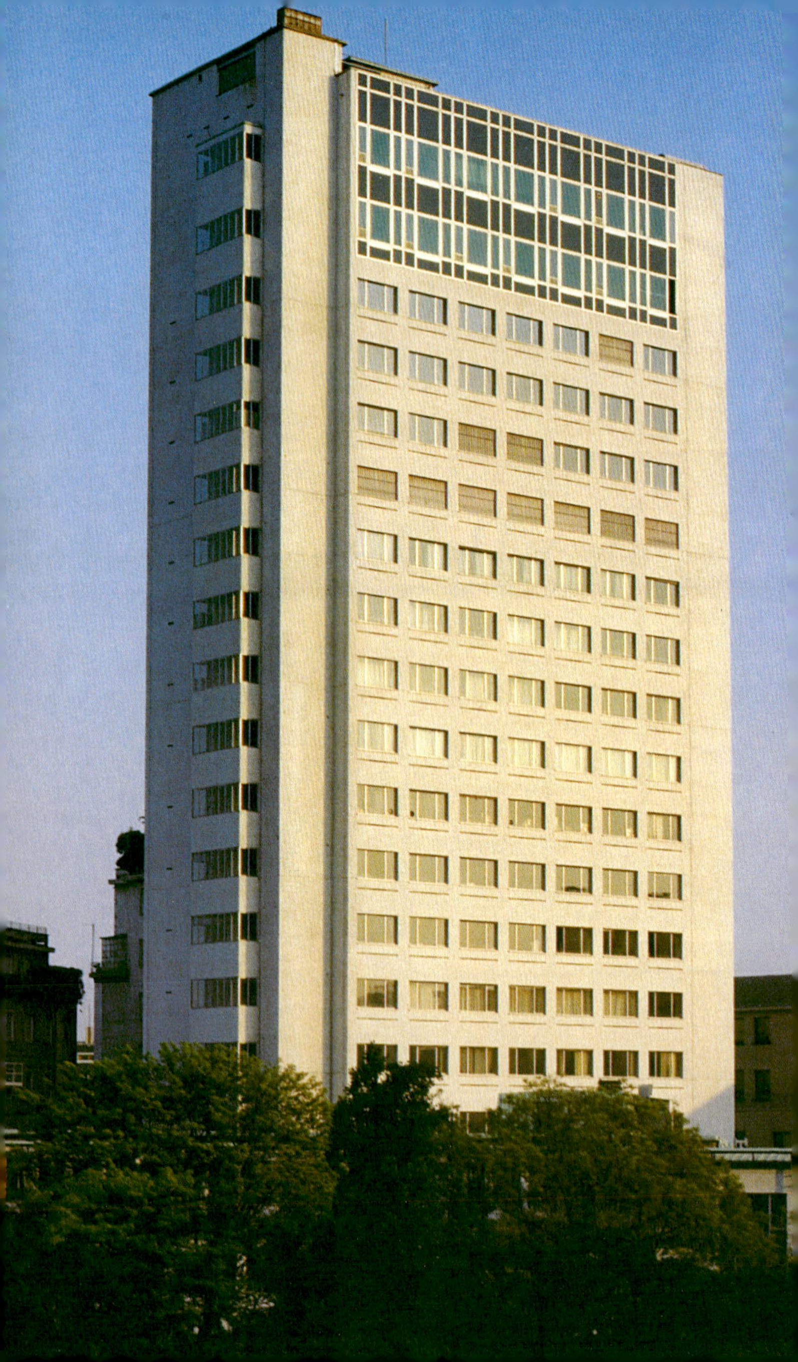

La Scala Opera House . . .

. . . and the nearby Sforza castle, Milan

Milan Pop. 1.5 million

There's little point in asking whether Milan is beautiful or ugly. Certainly you won't find the kind of beauty here that you find in Venice, Rome or Paris. What you will discover though is a city of so much interest and so many attractions as to be equalled by few others in the world. Even its quirks and its faults are appealing in their way.

The city doesn't flaunt itself as does, for instance, Rome. Milan is simply there, complete with its 1.5 million people whose industry, ambition and inventiveness are unique in Italy.

Milan's is a face you need to become accustomed to and your first impression may be little more than a blur. It can take time to bring things into focus. On the one hand the city is like a giant crucible into which beauty and ugliness are thrown together to re-emerge anew. On the other it is like a great forge turning out panettone and palazzi, monuments and high-rise blocks.

So this is Milan: possibly the most industrious city in Italy, probably the most dynamic, certainly the most elegant. Anyone who sees nothing more of it than the magnificent arcades at the city's heart, their shops and the passers-by has already seen a lot.

What better way of introducing this alluring city than through its fashion houses and boutiques (see pages 62–63), its restaurants and its bars (see pages 64–65)?

Left: High-rise development in central Milan

Style for all the world to follow

The expensive window displays beneath the glittering names of designers and fashion houses are immediately eye-catching. Many a shop with a branch in Bond Street or Fifth Avenue first opened here in the Via Monte Napoleone or one of the adjacent streets.

What can be so unique about the business flair of the Milanese? Why are so many people attracted to the capital of Lombardy from cities across Europe for a weekend buying and window-shopping? Even the staunchest Roman can't seem to resist a trip to the shopping arcades of Rome's rival in the north. Part of the explanation presumably lies in the way Milan displays its wares. This is a city where window-dressing is practised almost as an art, never simply to seduce the customer. Here the finest of merchandise is put stylishly on show with never a lapse into bad taste. All is elegance and restraint, everything just as it should be. *Rossetti* shoes and jewellery by *Bulgari* adorn the sparkling windows, but they do not beckon to you ostentatiously.

Laid out in barely one square kilometre of Milan is a dazzling Garden of Eden for would-be shoppers. Paradise begins in the *Via Monte Napoleone*. Since it costs upwards of 500,000 lire per square metre to rent a shop here only the very best can afford this exclu-

Fabulous fashion-shopping

sive location. World-famous names announce themselves from above the doorways: *Missoni* and *Ungaro*, *Gucci*, *Valentino* and *Galtrucco*. Sandwiched between them are the finest of shoe-shops and leather-boutiques, names like *Rossetti* and *Tanino Crisci*, *Beltrami* and *Ferragamo*.

Just as important for the image of this fabulous shopping street are its customers drawn from Milanese society. At every step you encounter elegant clothes by the best couturiers and the most famous ready-to-wear fashion houses. They are worn by leisured, well-groomed Milanese women shopping for *Mila Schön* skirts, jewellery or recordings of the opera, or perhaps for ham, cheese, meat pies and caviare, from delicatessens which seem almost ordinary by comparison but are nevertheless able to satisfy every whim.

The adjacent *Piazza San Babila* is bursting at the seams with Europe's most luxurious fashions for the young – colourful wind-cheaters in the most expensive of materials, American tennis shoes, and exclusive sun-tan lotions with conspicuous labels guaranteeing exorbitant prices.

Ready-to-wear fashions are also in evidence north of where the Via Monte Napoleone and the *Via Sant'Andrea* intersect. Here the little *Via della Spiga*, *Via Santo Spirito* and *Via Borgospesso* are enough to whet any appetite with tastefully dressed shop windows glinting from the façades of old 17th c. palazzi. The leaders of the Italian fashion trade, such as Giorgio Armani (with a shop in the Via Sant'Andrea and others in the Via Durini), work in this area, a 'Golden Triangle' in which *Trussardi* and *Ferré* are equally at home. *Cose* (Via della Spiga), *Adriana Mode* and *Marisa* (Via Sant'Andrea) are the best ports of call for women in search of classic clothes.

Among the specialities are cotton blouses and hand-embroidered linen. Of course you'll need to dig deep into your pocket, especially for anything with antique lace panels.

Gulp in the Via Santo Spirito specialises in more exotic fashions with creations which seem designed to cater for wealthy Arab taste: embroidered and printed oriental-looking velvets and silks, and tunics in voile. Shopping in Milan, it should be said, need not be fun only for the ladies. If you are looking for a silk tie or a super-smart dressing-gown, *Red & Blue* is the place to go for them, in the Via Monte Napoleone of course! Wool, silk and cashmere are the materials in which the man of fashion dresses in this elegant quarter. Stop off at *Etro* (Via Monte Napoleone and elsewhere), *Coveri* (Via San Pietro all'Orto) and *Boggi* (Piazza San Babila) to find them.

Of course, it must be said that one doesn't look for deals, bargains and discounts on fashion's golden mile between the Via Monte Napoleone and the Via Sant'Andrea!

There are a number of new little passages to explore where well-known designers are represented with their own boutiques. And you can recover from all the window-shopping in the *Caffè Moda Durini* in the Via Durini.

Remember that most shops and boutiques are closed during the lunchbreak. Shops only open again in the afternoon somewhere between 3 and 4 pm. This arrangement suits the Milanese, especially as the shops then stay open until about 7.30 pm. Even if you can't bring yourself to pay their kind of prices a stroll along the shopping arcades is still an experience. The quality of the merchandise is perfectly in keeping with the harmony of the buildings, a collocation of all the modern architectural styles.

Good food alla Milanese

After a successful shopping trip it'll hardly seem to matter if you spend a bit more! Treat yourself by going back to the Via Monte Napoleone to take the weight off your feet at one of the pretty tables in the *Caffè Cova* where elegantly dressed waiters in immaculate dinner-jackets serve cocktails, pastries and canapés. This is where Milan's well-heeled young gather in the evenings, mainly between 5 and 7 pm. Don't get the idea that these young people have no responsibilities in life other than being the sons and daughters of wealthy parents. Many of them are already launched into successful careers, working hard for publishing houses, as designers, or in the fashion world.

Enjoying an aperitif before meals is an Italian habit cultivated assiduously by the Milanese. The Galleria Vittorio Emanuele is a favourite venue for practising this pleasant ritual, *Down Town* and *Il Salotto* – both in the Galleria – being especially popular.

Milan enjoys as high a reputation for its food as for its fashion; in comparison with other cities the standards are well above average. Of course Milan today has become so cosmopolitan that it is no longer a particular stronghold of specifically Lombard cuisine. You can savour every culinary variation from across the length and breadth of Italy, from Italian interpretations of nouvelle cuisine to fortifying peasant dishes from southern Italy.

Where do people eat? Three names will feature at the top of any list: *La Scaletta*, *Savini* and *Gualtiero Marchesi*. More than mere restaurants, these are places of epicurean pilgrimage and you will have to pay accordingly. Not only are these temples to the art of eating

The Galleria Vittorio Emanuele by night . . .

Milan

absolutely first class, they are also quite small so it is advisable to book in plenty of time.

Real Milanese specialities are hard to find with only one or two restaurants keeping up the local culinary tradition. Anyone looking for genuine *Cotoletta alla Milanese* prepared and served in the original way should head for the Brera district and *Al Matarel* for example (leave your car in the garage and go by bus).

A bit of inside information for the summer: at the *Osteria del Binari* you can enjoy Lombard cuisine outside under a pergola. The meals are good and not too expensive.

Anyone in a hurry or wanting to keep hold of their lire will find plenty of places in Milan to eat quickly, reasonably, and also well. Try the self-service restaurants called *Ciao* for example.

Nowadays the places where people arrange to meet for a chat tend to be outside the city centre proper. If you're spending a few days in Milan set aside an evening to visit the *Brera district*, once the hub of Milan's artistic and intellectual life. Or visit the picturesque *Navigli quarter*, the old canal district near the Porta Ticinese (bus service). These corners of Milan have become very popular; everyone from the banker to the taxi-driver meets here. The atmosphere is friendly and informal, and there's less of a concern with status than you find in the city centre.

Two further tips: in the fifties and sixties the *Giamaica Bar* in the Brera district was a favourite meeting place for Milan's avant-garde painters. It's still a popular place today with a full house every evening. If on the other hand you're looking for a quiet corner in which you can talk in peace, try the *Posto di Conversazione*, a well-kept bistro in the Navigli quarter.

Addresses:

Caffè Cova, 8 Via Monte Napoleone.
Down Town, Galleria Vittorio Emanuele.
Il Salotto, Galleria Vittorio Emanuele.
La Scaletta, 3 Piazzale Stazione Porta Genova, tel. 58 10 02 90, closed Sun. and Mon.
Savini, 11 Galleria Vittorio Emanuele, tel. 86 46 05 35, closed Sun.
Gualtiero Marchesi, 9 Via Bonvesin de la Riva, tel. 65 42 04, closed Sun., and Mon. mornings.
Al Matarel, 2 Via Laura Solera Mantegazza, closed Tues.
Osteria del Binari, 1 Via Tortona, tel. 89 40 94 28, closed Wed. and Sat.
Ciao, 12 Corso Europa.
Giamaica Bar, 37 Via Brera, closed Sun.
Posto di Conversazione, 6 Alzaia Naviglio Grande.

. . . and by day

Milan's modern business park

The Milanese — hard-working and always one step ahead

What makes this great city so attractive is the feeling you get of always being a little ahead of the rest of the world in time — it is as if things happen here before anywhere else. A glance into the history books confirms it. The first trade unions were set up in Milan; the 'year of revolutions' (1848) saw its first uprising here; and Futurism was born around the tables of Milan restaurants.

Milan's most distinctive characteristic is its almost compulsive concern with *negotium* — Latin for occupation, trade or business. It is sometimes said in jest that the Milanese would be prepared to sell their cathedral if they could find anyone from outside the city silly enough to buy it! Still, without their legendary business acumen there would never have been a Milan trade fair, the shining symbol of Milan's industry and a fitting monument to Lombard

Futuristic football stadium

enterprise. The Milanese don't abuse their talents; they're proud of their reputation, proud of being the hub of Italian business life, the doyens of trade fairs and conferences, and unequalled in their commercial excellence and professionalism.

Milan's fashion houses are acknowledged to lead the world, ranked by the *cognoscenti* above even their rivals in Paris. Europe's top designers work here too, applying their incomparable flair for the imaginative and technically perfect use of shape and colour to everything from the most humble everyday items to the very finest ones. Milan's pre-eminent position in the media world and in publishing is also legendary. It is hardly surprising then that its people should sometimes appear somewhat arrogant and presumptuously confident of success, something the visitor gets used to only slowly.

It is hardly surprising either that with so much value assigned to business life the city has never attached great importance to its rich cultural heritage. Culture has always taken second place here, following in the train of technology and commerce, and even then for the most part only to bestow status and significance on what was happening in the factory. The 'Queen of Lombardy' is admired, envied and respected, but loved by only a few. Those few know however that behind the commercial mask of this enterprising city there is hidden a second intriguing face.

Exploring Milan

Setting out to explore the city it is easy to make a big mistake by taking one of the sightseeing buses which leave from the cathedral square. You'll pay a great deal of money to be accompanied by a local travel guide on what is supposed

Milan is world-famous for its fashion houses

to be a three-hour tour of Milan's sights and places of historic interest. The three hours, however, usually end up as two, because the guide hurries the driver round, especially in the afternoons. Often, moreover, your guide turns out to have an insufficient command of English, French or German for the commentary to be really understood.

If possible several days should be given over to exploring Milan on foot and to discovering the city's treasures for yourself.

The best place to start your sightseeing is at the *Piazza del Duomo*, the cathedral square. You can leave your car in one of the underground car-parks which are easily found (Piazza Diaz). The tourist information office is also here (corner of Via Marconi), and you can have a quick *cappuccino* in an espresso bar before you set off.

68 Milan

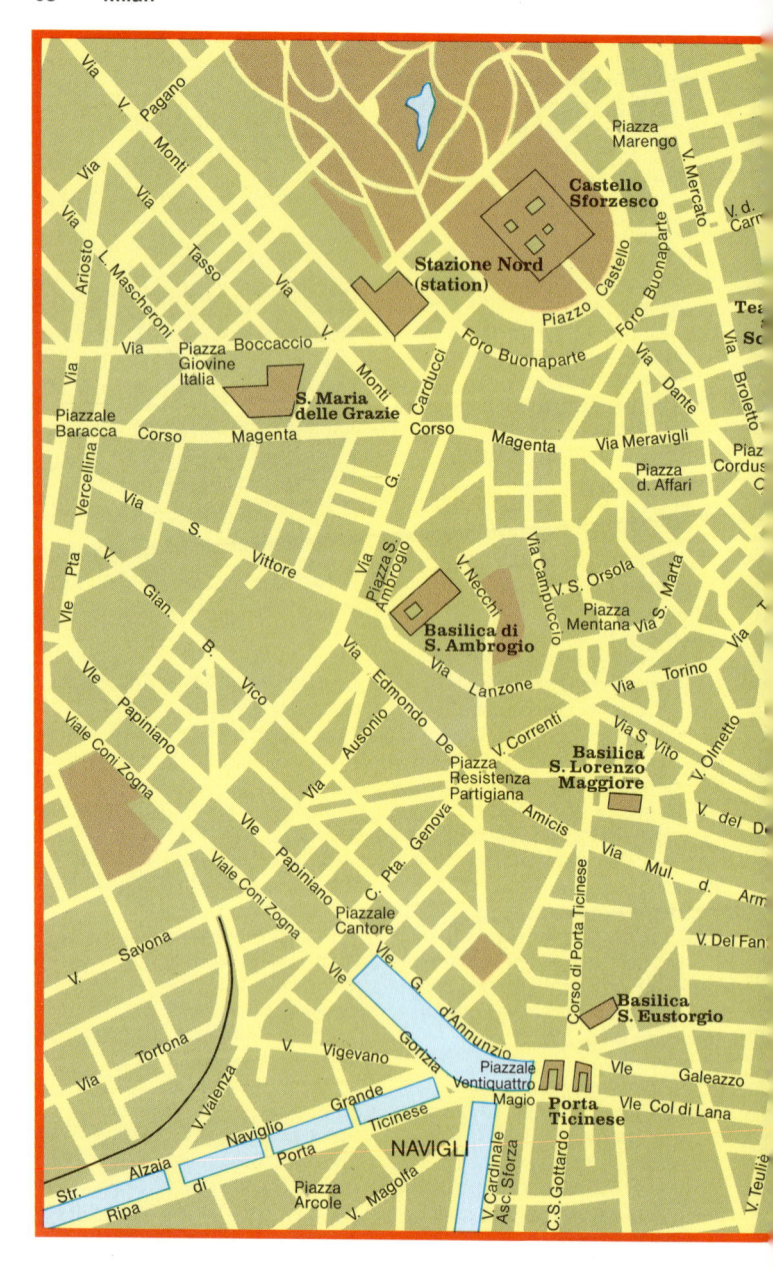

Milan 69

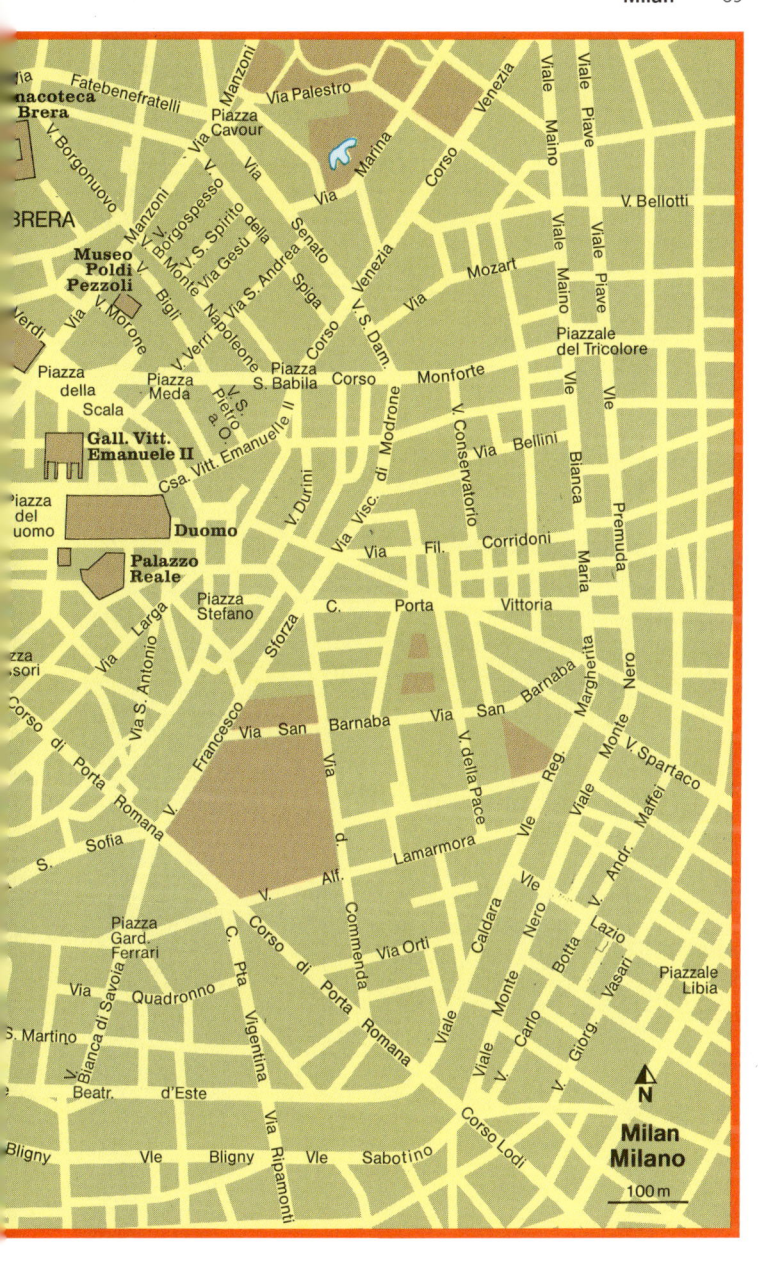

Duomo. The building of Milan Cathedral, from the laying of the foundations to the time the last statue was put in place, took its architects and stonemasons half a millennium. The foundation stone was laid in 1386. In the following centuries German, Italian and French architects carried on the work in the style of the Gothic cathedrals north of the Alps. The fine façade in a curious grey-pink marble was constructed between the 17th and 19th c.

The cathedral is beautiful – and enormous, as can be gathered from its statistics and dimensions. The roof is embellished with 135 spirelets, and 2,300 marble figures decorate the exterior (many of them unfortunately almost completely ruined by exhaust gases). The façade on the cathedral square is 68 m wide and 62 m high, and behind it the building is all of 158 m long. The cruciform base on which it stands has a total area of some 12,000 sq m. The cathedral is crowned by a lantern tower 108.5 m high. The central window of the

The roof and distinctive pinnacles of Milan Cathedral

choir is one of the largest Gothic windows in the world (22.5 m high and 11 m wide at the base). The interior is divided by fifty-two columns into five naves and three transepts.

After St Peter's in Rome Milan Cathedral is the largest church in Europe. The marble with which it is faced was brought by inland waterways from the Candoglia quarries near Ornavasso via Toce and Lake Maggiore, then along the Ticino and the Naviglio Grande to Milan.

Inside the cathedral a 'mystical darkness' reigns, produced by the many brightly coloured stained-glass windows. These mainly depict scenes from the Old and New Testaments, as well as some of the saints. The stained-glass work was carried out over a period stretching from the 15th to the 20th c.

The cathedral possesses a wealth of art works, most of them by artists who are scarcely known to the general public. One in particular who lived from 1527 to 1596 and worked as a painter, sculptor and architect stands head and shoulders above the rest: Pellegrino Tibaldi, who in addition to the façade also designed the floor mosaics, the tabernacle of the high altar and the choir stalls. Both the crypt leading to the tomb of St Charles Borromeo and the baptistry are also by Tibaldi.

Specially noteworthy are a *sundial* with the sign of Capricorn (at the beginning of the left aisle), the *tomb of Giacomo Medici* (one of Charles V's generals), the work of Leone Leoni (in the south transept; 1560–63), and the so-called *Trivulzio candelabrum*, a masterpiece of 12th c. French art (in the north transept).

Venice – the city on piles – is being washed away by the sea. Milan cathedral, which likewise rests on piles, is being undermined. The ground beneath it is subsiding because the tunnels for the *Metropolitana* (underground) were recklessly driven below it. In Venice the façades are crumbling because industrial pollutants are eating them away. The façade of Milan Cathedral is decaying for the same reason. Magnificent statues are disintegrating, the head of one Madonna having already fallen into the square. Restoration work is under way but the success of the undertaking remains in doubt. However, following a thorough cleaning the cathedral has a newly radiant appearance, and even the square in front of it is now clear of the building work associated with recent Underground improvements. As always it is well worth climbing up to the roof terraces, where you can enjoy a stupendous view over the city and as far as the Alps.

Palazzo Reale (12 Piazza del Duomo). Just to the right of the cathedral doorway stands the neoclassical Palazzo Reale (Royal Palace), built in 1778. Today it is used for art exhibitions. It also houses the *Museo del Duomo*, whose collection consists mainly of statues from the cathedral. Especially worth seeing is the early 15th c. statue of St George by Solari. (Open: 9.30 am–12.30 pm and 3–6 pm. Closed Mon.)

Galleria Vittorio Emanuele. If you now walk the 200 m across to the north side of the cathedral square you come to the entrance to this enormous city-centre shopping arcade built between 1865 and 1878. Each storey is 5 m high. Glass fronts on the ground floor are articulated by pilasters carried up through all the storeys. Ensconced behind the classy window displays in the covered arcades are dozens of elegant shops. Their façades flank passages almost 15 m wide, arranged in the shape of a cross and forming an octagon where they intersect. A huge glass

A special tip

Take a seat for an hour or two in the most beautiful 'salon' in Europe. From a table in one of the Galleria's cafés, or from one of its bars, you can watch the cast of passers-by 'perform'. Let your eyes wander over Mengoni's flawless, sumptuous architecture or, sipping your sparkling red aperitif, let fashionable Milan entertain you – stylish bankers and business people straight from the pages of *Vogue*, and chic Milanese women marvellously poised and well-groomed in their expensive, elegant, tasteful clothes. Even if you only stay long enough to drink a Campari it will still cost you about 15,000 lire! But it's worth it. Nowhere else will the Milanese introduce themselves to you in quite the same way.

barrel-vault roof carried on an iron framework covers the arcade. Even the eight-sided piazzetta is surmounted by a glass dome, with a diameter of 37 m. You can stroll here, dry whatever the weather, on the arcade's colourful mosaic parquet flooring.

The Teatro alla Scala is situated in the Piazza della Scala on to which the far end of the Galleria opens. *La Scala*! The name is full of magic for lovers of the opera, that bewitching realm of the musical world. The interior of the opera house is a kaleidoscope of velvet red, gold and ivory. This temple of Italian music looks actually quite modest from the outside but with 2,800 seats it is the largest theatre in Europe.

La Scala stands on the site of a church built 600 years ago by Beatrice della Scala, a member of the great Veronese Scaligeri family, in thanksgiving for God's gift of an heir. During the 18th c. the church fell into disrepair and the site was sold for a trifling sum to the leaseholders of the old ducal theatre who wanted to build a new opera house. Even as the work was due to begin many Milanese remained horrified that a theatre should be built on consecrated ground.

The Brera art gallery

Right next to La Scala is the *theatre museum* which houses a library of 65,000 volumes, an equally valuable music library, and memorabilia of Italian composers including Verdi, Rossini and Bellini. (The *Museo Teatrale alla Scala* is open daily except Sun., 9 am–noon and 2–6 pm; open Sun. also between May and September.)

The Museo Poldi Pezzoli (12 Via Manzoni) is only a short distance from the Piazza della Scala. You would hardly suspect that behind the severe façade of Count Poldi Pezzoli's former home (he died in 1879) is to be found probably the loveliest museum in Milan. Works of art collected by the Count over a period of decades are now exhibited in twenty-two (!) small rooms. They include works by Botticelli, Piero della Francesca, Perugino, Giovanni Bellini, Guardi, Tiepolo and Cranach the Elder. In addition there is porcelain, glass and enamelwork, as well as jewellery, clocks, bronzes and antique furniture. (Open: 9.30 am–12.30 pm and 2.30–6 pm, Sat. till 7.30 pm. Closed Sun. afternoon and Mon.)

Afterwards go back to the Piazza della Scala and then turn off into the Via Verdi, making your way along its continuation, the Via Brera.

Pinacoteca di Brera (28 Via Brera). Milan is often underestimated as a city of the arts. That it undoubtedly is a major centre is proved by the Brera, one of Italy's most important art collections, where more than 500 works are on exhibition, mainly by Italian masters of the 14th to the 20th c. Amongst them are masterpieces by Piero della Francesca, Benozzo Gozzoli, Andrea Mantegna, Giovanni Bellini, Vittore Carpaccio, Raphael and Titian. The Brera also owns Flemish works including paintings by Rubens and Van Dyck. (Open: 9 am–1.45 pm, Sun. 9 am–1 pm. Closed Mon.)

Now retrace your steps to the Piazza del Duomo and follow the Via Dante north-west to reach the Sforza castle in about fifteen minutes.

Castello Sforzesco (Piazza Castello). In 1450 building was started on a castle residence for the Sforza, the aristocratic Italian family who succeeded the Visconti as rulers of the duchy of Milan from 1450 until 1535. The site was previously occupied by a 14th c. castle belonging to the Visconti. The task of decorating the new castle was assigned to Bramante and Leonardo da Vinci. Later, especially during the 19th c., it fell into disrepair and was only restored to its former glory at the beginning of the 20th c.

Castello Sforzesco, which houses the city's art collection

Michelangelo's Pietà Rondanini, Castello Sforzesco

Today the city's *art collection* is housed in the Castello. Its most important work is the *Pietà Rondanini*, Michelangelo's last and strangest sculpture, which Milan acquired from Rome a few decades ago. It has a room to itself in the castle. (Open: 9.30 am–12.15 pm and 2.30–5.15 pm. Closed Mon.)

Milan's other places of interest cannot easily be reached on foot, so next you should take a bus from the Castello to the *Cimitero Monumentale*.

Cimitero Monumentale (Piazza del Cimitero Monumentale). The cemetery was laid out in 1866 on the north side of the city and extends over about 200,000 sq m. Its many magnificent tombs, monuments and chapels make it one of the most famous cemeteries in Europe.

From the cemetery take the bus again past the Stazione Nord railway station to one of Milan's loveliest Renaissance churches.

Santa Maria delle Grazie (Piazza Santa Maria delle Grazie). The building of this 15th c. church was begun to a Gothic design by the Italian architect Guiniforte Solari, but it was completed by Bramante at the end of the century in the Renaissance style. No one will want to miss visiting the refectory on the north side of the church, where Leonardo's world-famous painting *The Last Supper* (1495–97) is found. The fresco, measuring about 40 sq m and damaged soon after completion by dampness in the wall, has been restored a number of times, on occasion with inappropriate materials and by unsatisfactory methods. Whether this masterpiece can be preserved for posterity is as uncertain today as ever, despite the skilled restoration work of recent years.

The Last Supper was painted at a time of transition from Early to High Renaissance. Leonardo depicts the reaction of the disciples to Jesus' words 'One of you will betray me.' Breaking new ground in terms of composition the artist places the Apostles close to one another in four animated groups. For the first time Judas is not represented as isolated from the rest, nor is John pictured as leaning upon Christ.

The Basilica di Sant'Ambrogio (Piazza Sant'Ambrogio) is about fifteen minutes' walk away from Santa Maria delle Grazie, along the Via Carducci. It has endured much over the centuries after being founded in 374 by St Ambrose. Altered in the 8th and 11th c. and rebuilt from the 12th c. onwards, it underwent Gothic refurbishment in 1395, only to be renovated in keeping with Baroque fashion around 1630 and further altered and restored in the Romanesque style during the 19th c.

The church of St Ambrose is the most important in Milan. St Augustine is thought to have been baptised in the basilica by Ambrose, and in the Middle Ages it was here that the German emperors were crowned with the Iron Crown of Lombardy (see Monza).

Entrance to the church is through an atrium built in about 1150 following Early Christian models. Only a short distance inside, you are confronted by a pillar decorated with 13th c. frescos depicting St Ambrose, the Virgin Mary and one of the benefactors; beyond this are a classical column embellished with a serpent and an 11th c. pulpit with a relief of the Last Supper. Below the pulpit is a sarcophagus dating back to the 4th c., with scenes of Noah, Abraham, Elijah and Jesus.

Beneath a ciborium, the different elements of which date from various centuries, the high altar is adorned front and rear with 9th c. gold and silver panels further embellished with enamelwork and precious stones. These illustrate biblical episodes and scenes from the life of St Ambrose.

The mosaic in the apse – of Christ between the martyrs Gervase and Protasius – is less impressive than those of Saints Victor, Felix, Nabor, Maternus, Ambrose, Gervase and Protasius in the 5th c. *Sacello di San Vittore in Ciel d'Oro*.

The Basilica S. Lorenzo Maggiore, next on the itinerary, is reached via the Corso di Porta Ticinese. The *sixteen Late Classical pillars* gracing the forecourt were brought here in the 4th c. at the time of building. The basilica has been burnt down and rebuilt several times, the last being in the 16th c.

Its name does not in fact accurately reflect its design, the church being not a basilica but octagonal in shape. The interior resembles that of San Vitale in Ravenna.

Joined to S. Lorenzo is the *Cappella di Sant'Aquilino*. Two 4th c. mosaics in the chapel apse are particularly important since generally speaking very little survives from this period. One shows Christ with the Apostles, the other depicts the Translation of Elijah.

Monza Pop. 123,000

To complete the picture of Milanese art and culture you must drive the 15 km to Monza and visit the *cathedral* with its *Cappella di Teodolinda* (Theodolinda was sympathetic to Christianity while queen of Lombardy). The 'Iron Crown of the Lombards' with its decoration of gold and precious stones is kept in the altar tabernacle. Within the crown is a ring of iron, said to have been forged from a nail taken from Christ's cross. There are also memorabilia of Theodolinda: her copy of the gospels and a hen with seven chicks made of silver overlaid with gold – thought to symbolise the Lombard empire and its seven regions. In addition the *Museo Serpero* (open Tues.–Sat. 9 am–noon and 3–5 pm, Sun. and Mon. afternoons only) contains a wealth of beautiful things in ivory, gold, silver, quartz and silk.

Santa Maria delle Grazie

Panorama of Bergamo upper town

Historic towns in the shadow of the Alps

Anyone spending a holiday in northern Italy, visiting the lakes or Milan, should be sure not to miss four cities which many people regard as the most beautiful in the world: Bergamo, Brescia, Cremona and Mantua.

Bergamo Pop. 120,000

The Bergamo in question is in fact the *città alta* or upper town, visible from afar. The *città bassa* or lower town has been just as affected by the industrial development of the last few decades as have so many other cities of northern Italy.

Bergamo was first in Celtic hands before being seized by the Romans in 49 BC. As a free city in the 12th c. it was a leading member, along with Brescia and Cremona, of the Lombard League of cities which united against the Emperor Barbarossa. As early as the 15th c. Bergamo had become famous for its singing school. From the 17th to 19th c. it became equally well known for the manufacture of organs. Gaetano Donizetti (1797–1848), composer of seventy-four operas, the most important of which are *Lucrezia Borgia*, *The Love Potion* and *The Daughter of the Regiment*, was a student at Bergamo's school of music.

Around the cathedral square

Bergamo Alta is encircled by a mighty Venetian city wall which as it turned out was never required to withstand a siege. Enclosed within are a number of interesting buildings and other things to see. In the cathedral square, for instance, there is the *Colleoni Chapel*, a superb Renaissance building in coloured marble containing tombs of some of the powerful Venetian families. The dome of the chapel is decorated with frescos by the famous artist Giovanni Battista Tiepolo (1696–1770).

Also in the square the church of *S. Maria Maggiore* was begun in 1137, on the site of an earlier, Lombard church mentioned as long ago as 774. The three-aisled basilica has a high dome, erected in 1614, and an unusually large transept. The Gothic doorways and Baroque interior are well worth having a look at.

On the left-hand side, majestically completing the square, is the cathedral of *Sant'Alessandro* (15th c.). There are paintings by Tiepolo and Giovanni Battista Moroni (1530–78).

A stroll through the little streets of the Old Town is highly recommended.

Accademia Carrara. In *Bergamo Bassa*, the lower town, the Accademia Carrara is definitely worth a visit, having works by famous painters including Mantegna, Tintoretto, Carpaccio, Guardi and Tiepolo. (Open: daily 9.30 am– 12.30 pm and 2.30–5.30 pm. Closed Tues.)

A rack railway goes up to the Old Town.

International piano festival in May and June; Donizetti Festival in autumn.

Brescia Pop. 200,000

Brescia enjoyed little political good fortune in the Middle Ages and wisely placed itself under the protection of the Republic of Venice in 1426. Its motto seems today as apt as ever: 'Let others wage war; we shall provide armour and weapons.' First impressions are misleading. The impregnable-looking fortress looming over the city gives it an air of belligerent hostility, but in reality the Bresciani are more concerned with peace and prosperity. In the town centre a fitting balance is preserved between the sacred and the secular, with on one side the cathedral and elongated *Piazza del Duomo*, and on the other the city hall and *Piazza della Loggia*.

After Milan Brescia is the region's most important industrial and commercial centre. It still prides itself nevertheless on an impressive and well-preserved architectural heritage spanning every period.

From Antiquity to the Renaissance

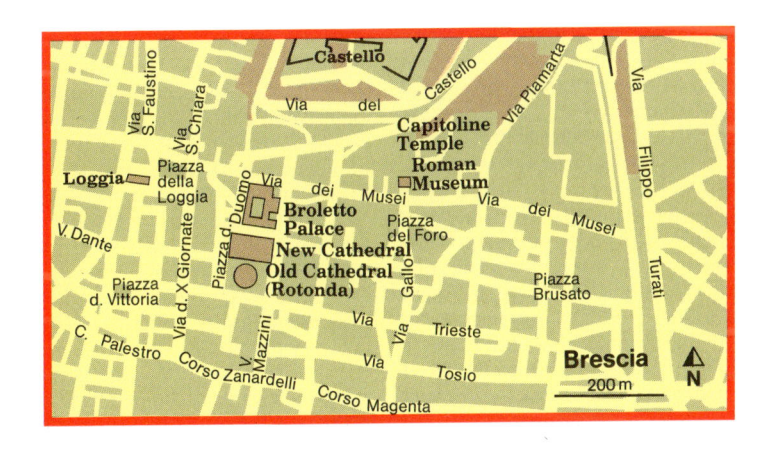

The so-called *Archaeological Zone* consists of the remains of a number of Roman buildings, among them the *Capitoline Temple* built by the Emperor Vespasian in AD 73. Archaeological finds dating back to the time when Brescia was called Brixia have been collected together to form the *Roman Museum*, adjoining the temple (open daily 9 am–noon and 2–5 pm; closed Mon.). They include the famous *Winged Victory* statue.

The centre of the medieval city, the *Piazza del Duomo*, is situated to the west of the ancient centre, only a few minutes away on foot. At the northern end of the Piazza stands the *Broletto Palace*, the town hall in medieval times, begun at the end of the 12th c., completed around 1230, and then enlarged in the 14th and 15th c. At the other end is the *Rotonda* (also known as the Old Cathedral), the most important Romanesque building in Brescia. It was constructed at the beginning of the 12th c., replacing the earlier basilica of S. Maria Maggiore (part of the mosaic floor of which still survives).

The exterior of the circular building is simple and unadorned, the interior being equally unpretentious. This serves only to heighten the effect. No other building in the whole of northern Italy provides a more perfect example or reveals more forcibly the inherent power of Lombard Romanesque architecture.

The *Piazza della Loggia* is a joy to behold. The heart of the city under Venetian rule, it provides a wonderful counterpart to the medieval Piazza del Duomo. Its crowning glory is the 16th c. town hall, called the *Loggia*, a superb Venetian Renaissance building covered with reliefs and decorative sculpture.

A special tip
Take time to wander through the alleyways behind the Loggia; they are as narrow as they are lively. In the space of a moment you feel yourself transported back through 500 years of history. On the other hand you also turn corners to find plain 18th and 19th c. façades which give no inkling of the still extremely well-preserved Late Gothic mansions behind them. Step into the old courtyards with their medieval arcades, narrow steps and tiny windows overgrown with flowers.

Cremona Pop. 80,000

Cremona is situated roughly half-way along the valley of the Po and is without question its most representative town. The people of Cremona are another industrious lot, earning a living mainly from textiles and agriculture. But it is its violin-makers who have carried the name of Cremona to all corners of the globe: this is the home town of Antonio Stradivari (1644–1737), the most famous of them all (see page 25). Cremona however is the birthplace not only of Stradivari and his equally famous colleagues Nicola Amati and Giuseppe Guarneri, who also made string instruments, but also of the composers Claudio Monteverdi (1567–1643) and Amilcare Ponchielli (1834–86).

Cremona's historic buildings date back to the Middle Ages, when it led the bold but difficult existence of an independent city state.

Romanesque architecture on a grand scale
Keep it to yourself, but the nicest place in Cremona is a seat in the peaceful *Bar Comune*, a coffee-house in an arcade

Historic towns in the shadow of the Alps

of the town hall, directly opposite the cathedral in the *Piazza del Comune*.

The *cathedral*, constructed over a period from the 12th to the 14th c., is a unique and truly monumental example of the Romanesque style in Lombardy. The galleried basilica with three naves is 68 m long, 31 m wide and 28 m high. Not to be missed on any account is the south façade dating from 1342, studded with wonderfully beautiful terracotta work. The frescos in the interior are mainly by 16th c. Cremona artists. Exceptions are a huge painting (1521) depicting Golgotha and another of *The Mourning of Christ* (1522), both works of considerable importance by the painter Pordenone from Friaul. In clear weather the platform of the *Torrazzo* offers a panorama embracing the whole of Cremona province – small wonder since at 111 m it is the highest campanile in Italy!

Opposite the cathedral stands the *Loggia dei Militi* built in 1292. With its arcade of pointed arches this is one of the loveliest Lombard Gothic buildings.

Cremona also steals the show with a number of outstanding palazzi from widely diverse stylistic periods. The most important are the *Palazzo Raimondi*, the Renaissance palaces *Stanga Trecco* and *Fodri*, and the *Palazzo Affaitati* which houses the town art gallery and the Stradivari Museum.

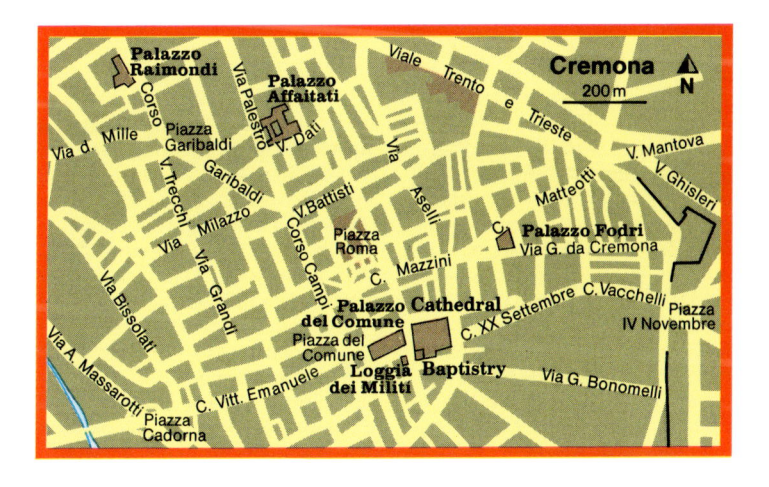

Piazza del Comune, Cremona

Ex Steamer excursion on the River Po

Cremona is the departure point for a most interesting steamer trip on the River Po (available March to May, and in September). In fact the m.v. *Stradivari* will take you as far as Venice if you wish. Details can be obtained from the *APT* (the provincial tourist office), 2 Galleria del Corso.

Mantua Pop. 57,000

Mantua is very proud of the poet Virgil, born in the village of Andes nearby. There is a monument to him in a garden in the Piazza Virgiliana. In contrast no one here shows much interest nowadays in the little imbroglio involving the French, Austrians, Bavarians and Italians in the days of Andreas Hofer, the Tyrolean freedom fighter who was court-martialled and shot in Mantua on Napoleon's orders in 1810. Perhaps that is rather too political for the administrators of this commercial centre.

Approached from the north by way of the San Giorgio bridge the town reveals its most strongly fortified side. Inside the walls, in the Piazza Sordello, the castle and cathedral stand in beautiful harmony. The people remain proud of their former rulers, the Gonzaga, who governed the city for almost four centuries from 1328 to 1708, making Mantua their seat. As a result it far outshone much larger towns in its art, and in cultural importance generally.

Until 1866 Mantua was alternately under French and Austrian rule.

The Ducal Palace – second only to the Vatican

In the medieval *Piazza Sordello* are the former residences of the Gonzaga family which together make up the huge *Palazzo Ducale* (Ducal Palace). Apart from the Vatican it is the largest palace complex in Italy. The late 13th c. palazzi belonging to the Bonacolsi family, which the Gonzaga appropriated when they took power, formed the nucleus of this ensemble of buildings which over the centuries grew to comprise more than 500 chambers and halls and numerous gardens. When visiting the palace be sure to take a guide; otherwise you are bound to lose your way in the confusing labyrinth of rooms (the Palazzo Ducale after all covers an area of 34,000 sq m!), and might miss the wonderful Mantegna frescos. (Open: Tues.–Sat. 9 am–1 pm and 2.30–4 pm, Sun. and Mon. 9 am–1 pm.)

Also in the Piazza Sordello is the *cathedral* which although begun in 1545 only acquired its façade in 1756. The ponderous campanile on the other hand dates from the 12th and 13th c. The interior of the cathedral represents an attempt to reconstruct the Early Christian type of five-naved basilica in the style of the Renaissance.

Rising high into the air in the Via Cavour is the *Torre della Gabbia*, so called because of the iron cage built half-way up it. Under the Gonzaga, who made a reputation for themselves as brilliant commanders in the field, condemned prisoners were put on show in the cage as a deterrent to others. In those days there would have been similarly high towers scattered all over the town, used by the city's warring families to defend themselves during the almost continuous rivalry and conflict.

The oldest of Mantua's historic buildings stands in what was the heart of the medieval town, the colourful and picturesque *Piazza delle Erbe* where daily markets are still held. The *Rotonda di S. Lorenzo* was built towards the end of the 11th c. by Matilda, Countess of Tuscany. The interior of this important early building is pure Italian Romanesque.

Historic towns in the shadow of the Alps 81

The Ducal Palace, Mantua – second only to the Vatican in size

The *Palazzo del Te* on the southern edge of the town is the most famous of all the architect Giulio Romano's designs, and was built and decorated as a retreat for Federico II Gonzaga between 1525 and 1535. The square, single-storey building opens on to a garden with an atrium where in 1530 the Emperor Charles V was received. Of the many pieces of stucco work by Romano and his assistants the finest are the life-sized figures of horses in the *Sala dei Cavalli* and the scenes from the myth of Cupid and Psyche in the *Sala di Psiche*. (Open: 9 am–6 pm. Closed Mon.)

Ex **By steamer on the Mincio**
During the summer months there are excursions by steamer on the River Mincio (information from the *APT*, 6 Piazza Andrea Mantegna).

Pavia Pop. 82,000

Situated on the banks of the Ticino, 35 km south of Milan, Pavia has managed to retain, at least in the heart of the town, its medieval charm. Splendid palazzi recall the great days of the old city state, which today is a pleasant university town engaged in trade and industry (and also in agriculture, in which rice plays a major role).

Pavia, originally called *Ticinum* and later *Papia*, was already a lively trading centre in Roman times. From the late 6th c. to the 8th c. it was the capital of the Lombards' north Italian empire. It was ruled by the Visconti family in the 14th c., and the castle, the *Castello Visconteo*, dates from this period. Today this houses the *municipal museums*; the art gallery contains important works by Foppa and Pisanello. (Open: varying times, according to the season; in summer and in December and January, mornings only, from 9 am–1 pm. Closed Mon.)

What to see

Pavia's most important buildings are in the Old Town, whose dense network of streets between the castle and the riverbank is partly pedestrianised. On the Piazza della Vittoria, the old marketplace with its attractive arcades, stands the *Broletto*, the 12th c. town hall. Near it is the Renaissance *cathedral*, and next to that, until recently, stood a massive medieval tower; it collapsed, but is to be rebuilt. Among Pavia's churches, the real gem is S. Michele, a fine Romanesque building erected in 1117 on the remains of a Lombard basilica, and which has an impressive sandstone façade with rich ornamentation. Dating from the same period, *S. Pietro in Ciel d'Oro* houses the tomb of St Augustine.

Do glance at the courtyards of the *university*, which was founded in the 10th c. and has been restored on several occasions (most recently by Piermarini, the architect of La Scala in Milan). Beyond it you can still see some of the town's once numerous medieval towers. A worthwhile walk takes you over the picturesque *Ponte Coperto*, a 14th c. covered bridge which was rebuilt after the War, to the fishermen's quarter on the other side of the Ticino.

Ex The splendid *Certosa di Pavia* (Carthusian monastery, 10 km north of the town) is one of the most beautiful Renaissance buildings in northern Italy. It was founded in 1396 by Gian Galeazzo Visconti, has a richly decorated, coloured marble façade, and houses many art treasures. The cloisters and monks' cells are especially charming. (Open: 9–11.30 am and 2.30–4.30 pm in winter; till 5 pm in spring and autumn, and till 6 pm in summer. Closed Mon.)

Another worthwhile excursion is to the old bridge over the Ticino at *Bereguardo*. There are good fish dishes to be sampled in the restaurants in the vicinity. Further to the west, surrounded by ricefields, is *Vigevano* with its wonderful Renaissance arcaded square attributed to Bramante and Leonardo. Vigevano is also a good place to buy shoes, since over a third of Italy's shoe production comes from the town. Connoisseurs of wine will certainly want to make the trip to the vineyards of the *Oltrepò Pavese*.

Lake Iseo

Lake Iseo

Even at 25 km long, with an average width of 2.5 km and a surface area of at least 62 sq km, Lake Iseo has a great deal of competition, overshadowed as it is by Lake Garda on the one hand and Lake Como and Lake Maggiore on the other. Many tourists seem quite unaware of the existence of this enchanting stretch of water situated in between. The Romans knew about it, however, and called it *Lacus Sebinus*.

It is a peaceful place, nestling almost unobtrusively between the Camonica Valley and the wine-growing area of Franciacorta. Its western shore belongs to the province of Bergamo, its eastern one to Brescia. The River Olgio flows through it, entering near Pisogne in the north-east corner and leaving again between Sarnico and Paratico in the furthest south-west.

Anyone driving round the lake – a trip of two hours at most – will soon become aware of its close resemblance to Lake Garda. Here as on Garda the *Ora* blowing from the south ruffles the blue-green waters of the lake, and in the north the winding lakeside road from Lovere hugs the steep mountainsides just as closely as does the corresponding road along Lake Garda.

Lake Iseo, also referred to as Sebino after its Latin name, even has its own undisputed jewel in the crown. Picturesque Monte Isola, the largest island in any Italian lake, lies just about in the middle, 3 km long and rising to 600 m. Its slopes are densely wooded with chestnut-trees.

Although Sebino's waters are clearer and cleaner than, for instance, Lake Garda's or parts of Lake Como, its attractions are yet to become widely known north of the

Alps. It has to be said that there is not as yet much in the way of experience to draw on in the tourist offices around the lake, but for some years now the local councils have been making a real effort to lift themselves and Lake Iseo out of the shadows and into the warm sunshine of a growing tourist trade.

The typical Lake Como holidaymaker will doubtless not feel at home on Lake Iseo. The climate will not be Mediterranean enough nor the resorts fine enough, nor will there be found the same wide-ranging choice of large hotels. To such a visitor everything about Lake Iseo seems wilder and far less gentle in comparison. And so indeed it is. But, by the same token, nobody who chooses Lake Iseo for its natural and untamed beauty would ever dream of heading off for the mellowed Mediterranean perfection of the other holiday lakes. Furthermore, Sebino is still very reasonable, which will recommend it especially to young holidaymakers and families with children. Prices are not too high in either the hotels and pensions or the restaurants.

The lake is a paradise for anglers, being one of the most abundantly stocked of all the lakes in northern Italy. It is also the nearest lake for trippers from Bergamo and Brescia, so in August especially the approach roads are often packed with traffic. And as you do the circuit of Sebino on the scenic lakeside road you could be forgiven for thinking that there are more campsites than hotels.

Paratico Pop. 3,000

After you leave the Milan-Venice motorway at Palazzolo, Paratico is the first village you come to. It is spread out over concentric terraces climbing the slopes of the surrounding hills. Its main landmark is the ruined *Castello Lantieri* in which Dante is reputed to have stayed.

Iseo Pop. 10,000

Named after the lake, Iseo is a friendly place. It has two special attractions, its ancient town centre and the roomy and exceptionally well-designed 'Sassabanek' swimming complex.

Just south of Iseo there is an extensive area of peat bog rich in beautiful wetland flora. The remains of prehistoric pile dwellings have been found there. A reputation for traditional fish recipes brings many an appreciative gourmet to neighbouring *Clusane* where the imposing 14th c. *Carmagnola Castle* can also be seen, perched on a nearby hill.

Be sure to have a look at the 12th c. church of *S. Andrea* with its

Romanesque campanile. Inside is a painting, the *Archangel Michael*, a major work by the artist F. Hayez. Equally worth seeing is the little church of *S. Maria del Mercato* decorated with 13th and 14th c. frescos.

In and around Iseo there are numerous bathing places in the lake. It is so shallow here that you can sometimes stand 100 m from the shore and still be only up to your hips in water. As a result, though, the water is often so warm (particularly in August) that it ceases to be refreshing. Ideal for children.

The magnificent *Sassabanek* swimming and sports centre is absolutely outstanding. You can refresh yourself in any one of several beautifully kept swimming pools and sunbathe on the vast lawns which extend right down to the lake shore.

Rowing boats and pedalos for hire.

There are numerous campsites around the town. Reasonable prices bring holidays here within the means of the younger generation of tourists in particular.

Ex Fine wine and monasteries

To the south of Lake Iseo there stretches an area of gently undulating hill country known as the *Franciacorta*, a landscape of vineyards, woodland, ancient castles and old manor houses. Here neither the still nor the sparkling wines suffer the indignity of adulteration; on the contrary, they are celebrated the world over for their excellence. But the Franciacorta has its cultural treasures too, and you should

Iseo harbour

make a point of stopping to see the abbey at *Rodengo Saiano* as well as the monastery of *San Pietro* in Provaglio and the convent of the *Holy Annunciation* in Rovato.

Sulzano Pop. 1,300

This little place could have been made specially for sailing and other watersports, so it is just as popular with local people as holidaymakers. With its quaint houses, narrow little alleys and pretty pergolas the village is sandwiched between the lake and the mountains. From here you can make the short crossing to the island of Monte Isola.

Ex There is excellent walking in the surrounding hills with splendid views of the lake. Highly recommended.

Sale Marasino Pop. 3,000

Sale Marasino huddles directly below a mountain ridge, its houses finding a foothold on the lower, gently rising slopes. The church of *S. Zenone* in the centre of the town is exceptionally fine with some lovely frescos. Close beside the lake the 16th c. *Villa Martinengo* is surrounded by a lush garden. Also of interest is the Renaissance-style mansion of the Dossi-Giugni family.

Monte Isola Pop. 2,000

Numerous boats run regular services to the island from various lakeside towns and villages. On this, the largest island in any Italian lake, shady woods alternate with sunny expanses of green. This is a landscape of fishing villages and of farms nestling between olive-groves, chestnut-trees and vines. All vehicles are banned except for some public transport. Monte Isola is as if in a time warp, in another world.

From atop an already towering cliff the walls of the *Oldofredi-Martinengo* castle (14th to 16th c.) rise even higher into the sky, while in Siviano there is another former Martinengo possession, a medieval tower. One of the remote bays conceals the 16th c. *Villa Ferrata*, and at the island's highest point (600 m) you find the small pilgrim church of *Madonna della Ceriola*. From up there the view takes in the entire lake, complete with the tiny islands of Loreto and S. Paolo.

Despite its great beauty Monte Isola will strike most people as a place for an excursion rather than a longer stay. Except for a campsite at the foot of the wooded peak, overnight tourist accommodation is limited to a handful of small pensions.

Zone Pop. 1,100

Encircled by woods of pine and beech, Zone lies in an evergreen-clad valley at the foot of Monte Guglielmo (1,945 m). You reach it from Marone. With wonderfully wild scenery all around it Zone is an ideal base from which to go walking. Near the neighbouring village of *Cislano* you come across curious earth pinnacles pointing skywards. These slender pillars up to 30 m high are capped with flat boulders. Thousands of years of erosion have sculpted them from a glacial moraine.

Zone has a number of churches with interesting interiors. Especially worth seeing, for instance, is the 12th c. parish church of *S. Giorgio* which has lovely 16th c. frescos. And while you are here don't forgo the opportunity to visit the two little churches of *S. Cassiano* and *S. Antonio*.

Good food in the *Pizzeria Almici* in the Via Caporotondo.

Pisogne Pop. 8,000

Pisogne is a little town of many faces where the contrast between lake and mountains is at its starkest. Centuries old, it is still full of relics from the past.

The *Piazza Corna Pellegrini* is a delight, ringed by distinguished buildings and arcades.

Definitely worth seeing is the church of *S. Maria della Neve*, often referred to as the poor man's Sistine Chapel on account of Girolamo Romanino's delightfully coloured and marvellously expressive frescos.

In another part of the town, the area known as *Grignaghe*, there are fragments of statues dating from the Lombard period.

Ex In the Palotto valley above Pisogne extensive woods and gently sloping meadows provide lots of opportunities for walking. From *Fraine*, a summer resort some 9 km north-east of Pisogne, you can enjoy an impressive panoramic view of the lake.

Lovere Pop. 6,000

Although not in quite so lovely a setting as the resorts further south on the lake,

Lovere has plenty of attractions to offer its visitors. The medieval town centre is richly endowed with historic buildings. The people of Lovere are enterprising craftsmen and successful in commerce. Although the town is not an ideal base for tourists the local council has succeeded in wooing a mainly Italian clientele who faithfully return year after year.

Anyone with an interest in art should certainly look round the 19th c. *Palazzo Tadini*, which boasts a comprehensive art collection with works by Italian masters as well as collections of valuable sculpture, ceramics and old armour. A series of concerts is held there every year.

The remains of the *Castello Gallico* at the foot of Monte Cala provide an impressive reminder of Lovere's ancient origins.

Sailing club and sailing school.

Ex Worthwhile detours from the lakeside road

The western shore of Lake Iseo between Lovere and Sarnico offers several rewarding detours and walks. The lakeside road itself is very picturesque in places, cutting through steep walls of rock. South of Lovere, the narrow gorge near *Castro* and the ravine at *Zorzino* are both impressive. You reach the latter from the fishing village of *Riva di Solto*. The little towns and villages on the hills all around you, for example *Bossico* inland from Lovere, and *Fonteno* further south, afford superb views over the lake and mountains. In *Predore*, a peaceful and well-appointed lakeside resort a few kilometres before Sarnico, the swimming pool at the holiday development is a tempting place to pause for a rest.

Sarnico Pop. 5,500

Sarnico is one of the few really lively and busy towns on Lake Iseo. The remains of a pile settlement are proof that human beings have lived here from the very earliest times, while the ruined castle and fortress walls are relics from the town's medieval days. Today the manufacture of confectionery plays an important part in the economy of this health resort, and Sarnico is known throughout the world for the boats of all sizes built in its yards. The town has also hosted waterskiing championships.

The town centre has a charm of its own, inviting leisurely walks along the shady lakeside promenade and through its welcoming pergolas.

Sailing club and sailing school.

Simple honest Italian cooking at *Al Tram* on the Piazza Matteotti; excellent salmon trout at the hotel restaurant *Il Cantiere*.

Lake Idro

Lake Idro suffers like Lake Iseo from being too little known. Indeed it is even more eclipsed by Lake Garda than is its neighbour further west. Even so, the travel companies have worked hard to ensure that it attracts at least a small band of devotees, many of them foreign.

Lake Idro has an area of 11 sq km, is 122 m deep and at 468 m above sea-level is the highest of all the lakes in Lombardy. With a lively river, the Chiese, flowing through it, Idro proved suitable for use as a reservoir, so as well as being a tourist attraction this peaceful, rather sleepy lake performs two other valuable functions: water is drawn from the dam to power an electricity-generating station, and the dry plains of Mantua and Brescia are irrigated from it during the summer months.

Don't expect tourist-style hotels on this 10-km-long lake. Such facilities as there are are mainly for anglers, Lake Idro far exceeding even Lake Iseo in the abundance of its fish. Also, since it is wedged in a narrow valley the lake is inevitably restricted in the amount of daily sunshine it receives, so the water is never warmer than 19°C/66°F. But it still offers a refreshing bathe and you won't find any signs of pollution. Its virtues indeed are now beginning to be appreciated by windsurfers seeking refuge from overcrowded Lake Garda.

Idro. On its eastern side the wooded mountains plunging steeply to the lake barely leave room for human habitation. Only Idro and Crone squat together in the southernmost corner. At one time nails were forged in Idro using ore from the iron deposits found in the area, as they also were in nearby Val Trompia which separates Lakes Iseo and Idro. The nails, absolutely indispensable in those days, were already being manufactured here during the period of Venetian rule, and even anchors for the Venetian fleet were made here. Output from the naileries was later put to more peaceful use in the manufacture of wooden-soled sandals.

In *S. Maria in Undas* there are carvings worth seeing, as well as a fine statue of the Madonna.

S. Antonio and Anfo. The road which runs high above the lake along its western shore can lay claim to only two villages – S. Antonio and Anfo. Anfo, overhung by rock, boasts a mighty fortress built by the Venetians in 1483. This impregnable bastion was further strengthened by Napoleon, and in the spring of 1945 took on new strategic importance during the German retreat.

A total of eleven campsites have been set up around Lake Idro, three to the east of Idro at the southern end, the remainder on the west side north and south of Anfo.

If camping doesn't appeal you could stay instead in one of the holiday chalets. Most are on the outskirts of Anfo, near the campsites.

Since prices are very reasonable on Lake Idro more and more young people have taken to holidaying there in recent years. But the lake is just as well suited to anyone who prefers beautiful scenery and remoteness to the attractions of an already fully developed holiday area.

Useful things to know

Before you go
Climate
Variations in the weather should be taken into account because although the lakes are part of the same region, their climate is quite different from that in the rest of Lombardy.

The prevailing climate on the plain of Lombardy is transitional, with severe winters and hot summers. Daytime temperatures can vary considerably. From December to February the average lowest temperatures are between −2°C/28°F and −5°C/23°F. In spring and autumn − the best times to travel − the mean daily maximum is 18°C/64°F in April and October, 24°C/76°F in May and September. In summer, temperatures of 28°C/82°F to 31°C/88°F can normally be expected. On average there are 1,911 hours of sunshine a year. There is no shortage of precipitation, however; Milan for example registers an annual mean of about 900 mm. Snow falls frequently in winter. Drivers need to be forewarned about the notorious winter fogs in the Lombard plain; they are extremely dangerous.

Around the big lakes, on the other hand, things are very different. The huge quantities of water stored in them ensure that summers are not too hot and winters not too cold − the temperature rarely falls below 0°C/32°F. The result is a lushness of vegetation of a kind more usually found further south. On Lakes Como and Maggiore palms comfortably survive the winter out of doors. Especially in the summer months violent thunderstorms and rain-showers can be expected in the evenings (though these seldom last for more than about an hour).

A little geography
Lombardy is situated in the north-west of Italy. On its north side it shares a common frontier with Switzerland. It is bordered in the west by Piedmont, in the south by Emilia-Romagna and in the east by Veneto and Trentino-Alto Adige. With an area of 23,856 sq km it is the fourth largest of Italy's regions, after Sicily, Piedmont and Sardinia. Even so the Lombardy region occupies barely 8% of the total area of Italy. About 9 million people, or over 15% of Italians, live there, 1.5 million of them in Milan.

Lombardy divides geographically into three areas. In the north is the Alpine chain, its highest mountain being Pizzo Bernina (4,052 m). These high Alps merge into the hilly pre-Alps. It is here that the lakes of Lombardy are found, lying in large basins scoured out over an extended period long ago by glaciers. Finally, in the south the valley of the Po borders on the Apennines. The Po Valley or north Italian lowland plain forms, incidentally, the only low-lying area of any significance in the whole of the Apennine peninsula.

Getting to the Italian lakes
By air: There are scheduled flights to Milan and Turin from all major cities, and charter flights are also available. In addition there are convenient fly-drive packages allowing you to fly to the Lombard capital, for example, and drive on immediately to Lake Como or Lake Maggiore. Full information is available from travel agents.

By rail: There is a direct rail service from London Victoria to Milan. In Italy itself the railways are efficient and travel costs agreeably low.

A particularly attractive system operates whereby travellers not resident in Italy can buy tickets at the frontier allowing unlimited rail travel anywhere on the peninsula. These tickets are valid for between eight and thirty days.

By road: Distance apart, going to the Italian lakes by car poses few problems. Northern Italy has an extremely efficient road network. Its main traffic arteries are the toll motorways; you pay in cash or with a *Viacard* (obtainable from tollbooths, some banks, tourist offices and tobacconists), the amount charged depending on distance travelled and size of vehicle. Toll-booths are usually installed on approach and exit roads.

The principal recommended route to northern Italy from the UK is via the Mont Blanc Tunnel. Further information is available from the RAC Routes Department (address on page 94). Whichever route is chosen, car sleeper services will shorten the driving time; information from the French or Belgian state railways.

Information about road and traffic conditions, routes, etc. within Italy is obtainable from the Italian automobile club (ACI) which has offices in nearly all major Italian cities.

Immigration and customs regulations

Customs: Luggage and personal effects including e.g. 2 cameras and 10 films, a video camera and 10 films, portable radio, portable musical instrument, portable tape-recorder and television set, typewriter and binoculars, camping and sports equipment may be taken into Italy duty free. Goods of no commercial value such as food also incur no duty.

For EC residents, the usual allowances for goods obtained duty paid in the EC apply on entry. Tobacco products: 300 cigarettes or 75 cigars or 400 g tobacco; alcoholic drinks: 5 litres of wine and 1.5 litres of spirits over 22% or 3 litres of spirits up to 22%; other goods: 1 kg coffee, 200 g tea, 75 g perfume. The same allowances apply on departure.

Duty-free allowances: 200 cigarettes or 50 cigars or 250 g tobacco; 1 litre of spirits over 22% or 2 litres up to 22%, and 2 litres of wine.

Non-EC visitors should check allowances with their tour operator.

Travel documents: British visitors to Italy require only a valid passport or a British Visitor's Passport. US and Canadian visitors also require only a passport. A visa is needed only for stays exceeding 3 months.

Though it is not obligatory motorists are advised to obtain an international 'green card' insurance certificate to avoid lengthy discussions at police controls. In addition they need a valid driving licence and registration documents.

During your stay
Currency

There are no restrictions on the import of foreign currency into Italy, though the amount taken out on leaving the country may not exceed the amount taken in. Italian money may be taken out only to a maximum of 500,000 lire; there is no restriction on the amount taken in.

Currently in circulation are banknotes in denominations of 100,000, 50,000, 10,000, 5,000, 2,000 and 1,000 lire as well as coins of 500, 200, 100, 50, 20, 10 and 5 lire. The 100,000 and 50,000 lire banknotes are legal tender only in Italy, not abroad. The grooved telephone tokens (*gettoni*) may also be tendered in lieu of cash (200 lire).

Eurocheques to a value of 300,000 lire each can be changed in banks, bureaux de change and many hotels. The major credit cards are accepted in many places.

Exchange rates are published in the national press, or can be obtained from banks.

Electricity

Italy is gradually converting to a standard 220 volts. At present voltages still vary from 110 to 220 volts (you can see which from the lightbulbs). Italian sockets (*presa*) do not normally take the standard UK or US plugs so an adaptor (*adattore*) is needed (obtainable from electrical shops or, better still, before departure).

Hotels and pensions

There are considerable seasonal price differences in all hotels between the early and late season on the one hand and the high season on the other. Italy has five categories of hotel and pension (luxury or five-star down to one-star). These categories give only a rough indication of standards. If you strike lucky a hotel with three stars may be better than one with four. The overnight, half-board and full-board tariffs must be clearly displayed in the hotel room (usually on the back of the door or wardrobe door). Ask about reductions for children too.

Insurance

In Italy medical care is of a high standard. UK citizens are covered for minor illnesses under an EC agreement (a form E111 should be obtained from the DSS or a post office before leaving home). This certificate must be exchanged at the Italian health department, *USL*, for a voucher entitling you to treatment. USL offices can be found in every largish town. It is also advisable however to take out additional medical insurance.

Comprehensive travel insurance covering third-party liability, health, accidents and luggage is available from travel agencies and at airports. British motorists may obtain RAC Eurocover insurance from RAC offices, or by contacting the Croydon office (address on page 94).

Opening times

Banks normally open on weekdays from 8.30 am to 1.30 pm and from 3–4 pm. On Saturdays, Sundays or public holidays you can change money at the bureaux de change at stations in the larger towns or at airports. Milan has a few exchange machines.

Museums, churches and archaeological sites close over the lunch break from noon to 3 pm, and most are closed all day on Mondays. Entrance to some museums is free on Sundays.

Petrol stations usually close between noon and 3 pm (except for those on the motorways). Look out for the signs *aperto* (open) and *chiuso* (closed). In the evening the pumps usually close down some time between 7 and 8 pm.

Shops are normally open Monday to Friday from 8.30 or 9 am to 12.30 pm, and from 3.30 to 7 or 7.30 pm. Of course in the popular holiday resorts on the lakes many shops stay open till 10 or 11 in the evening (and also open on Sundays and holidays) to capture the holiday trade.

Post and telephone

Post offices (*posta* or *ufficio postale*) handle telegrams, post, and money transactions. Many have public telephones. Stamps can also be bought from tobacconists (*tabacchi*) and sometimes from hotel reception desks. Post-

Useful things to know

Typical post-boxes

boxes are striped red. Post offices are normally open on Mondays to Saturdays from 8.30 am to 7 pm.

Telephone *(telefono)* calls abroad are best made through an operator at a main post office in one of the larger towns. Hotels will also arrange long-distance calls, of course, but this is more expensive. Either way the international lines are frequently overloaded so be prepared for a long wait. In Italy the public telephone service (SIP) is separate from the postal services. Coin-operated public telephones use their own grooved tokens *(gettoni)* in units of 200 lire dispensed from special change-machines. Restaurants and shops which have a public telephone display a sign with a black disc on a yellow background. Many telephones take both gettoni and coins, and also telephone cards *(schede telefoniche)*, obtainable from bars, tobacconists and newspaper kiosks. To telephone abroad dial 0044 for Britain (01139 for the US/Canada), the area code minus the initial 0, and finally the subscriber number.

Public holidays
New Year: January 1st
Epiphany: January 6th
Easter Monday
Liberation Day: April 25th
Labour Day: May 1st
Feast of the Assumption: August 15th
All Saints: November 1st
Immaculate Conception: December 8th
Christmas: December 25th and 26th

In addition there are regional holidays when once again the banks and shops are closed.

Receipts
Foreign visitors often forget that they may be required to produce a receipt *(ricevuta fiscale)* for services rendered. This even includes receipts from hotels and restaurants, not just for things like car repairs. Bear in mind that you could face a fine if you cannot produce your receipts at one of the checks carried out by Italian tax officials.

Time
Italy keeps Central European Time (GMT + 1 hour). Clocks are advanced a further hour in summer, an hour ahead of British Summer Time.

Tipping
Hotels and restaurants generally add a fixed service charge to the bill (between 10 and 15%). Staff expect this sum to be added to, however, and failure to do so will be taken as an expression of dissatisfaction.

As a rule of thumb, a tip of 20,000 lire each for the waiter and chambermaid is about right after fourteen days in a medium-range hotel. For all other services (e.g. hairdressers and taxis) tips of 10 to 15% are expected.

Traffic regulations, motoring
Vehicles travel on the right. Seat belts must be worn in front seats, and children aged 4 to 10 must occupy seats with seat belts or other restraining device. Vehicles must be fitted with an outside mirror on the left side and a nationality plate on the back. It is also

obligatory to carry a warning triangle and a spare set of bulbs for lights and indicators.

In towns, traffic coming from the right has priority. In the country, main-road traffic has priority unless signs show otherwise. Drivers must signal their intention to change lanes or overtake. In town the horn should only be used in an emergency. Do not drink and drive; penalties are severe.

Fuel for private motor vehicles must only be carried in the tank fitted to the vehicle. For safety reasons it is forbidden to carry spare fuel and to fill fuel cans at a petrol station. Petrol tokens offering tourists a discount on the normal price of petrol can be purchased at frontier crossing-points, or from RAC offices (personal callers only). Information about petrol stations stocking lead-free petrol (*benzina senza piombo*) is available from RAC offices, or telephone RAC Touring Information (081 686 0088).

Speed limits: built-up areas 31 mph (50 kph), outside built-up areas 56 mph (90 kph). Motorway speed limits vary according to engine size. Cars up to 1090 cc/motorcycles up to 349 cc: 68 mph/110 kph; cars over 1100 cc/motorcycles over 349 cc: 81 mph/130 kph. Cars towing caravans are limited to 50 mph/80 kph outside built-up areas and 62 mph/100 kph on motorways.

Important addresses
Diplomatic and consular offices

British Embassy
80a Via XX Settembre
00187 Roma;
tel. 06/4 755 441, 4 755 551

British Consulate
7 Via San Paolo
20121 Milano;
tel. 02/803 442

United States Embassy
119a Via Vittorio Veneto
00187 Roma;
tel. 06/4 674

United States Consulate
32 Piazza Repubblica
20124 Milano;
tel. 02/6 528 415

Australian Embassy
215 Via Alessandria
00198 Roma;
tel. 06/832 721

Canadian Embassy
27 Via G. B. de Rossi
00161 Roma;
tel. 06/841 341

Irish Embassy
3 Largo del Nazareno
00187 Roma;
tel. 06/6 782 541

New Zealand Embassy
28 Via Zara
00198 Roma;
tel. 06/4 402 928

Tourist information offices
In UK
Italian State Tourist Office (ENIT)
1 Princes Street
London W1R 8AY;
tel. 071 408 1254

In United States
Italian State Tourist Office
630 Fifth Avenue, Suite 1565
New York, NY 10111;
tel. 212/245 4822–24

In Italy
First-rate information is provided by the tourist agencies found in every large town or city:

APT – Azienda di Promozione Turistica
Bergamo: 106 Viale Papa Giovanni, tel. 242 226
Brescia: 34 Corso Zanardelli, tel. 43 418
Como: 17 Piazza Cavour, tel. 262 091

Cremona: 5 Piazza del Comune, tel. 23 233
Milan: 1 Via Marconi, tel. 809 662
Varese, 9 Viale Ippodromo, tel. 284 624
Mantua: 6 Piazza A. Mantegna, tel. 350 681
Pavia: 2 Via Fabio Filzi, tel. 22 156

In addition all kinds of information may be obtained from local tourist offices and the administrative offices of individual resorts *(Azienda Autonoma di Soggiorno)*.

RAC
RAC Motoring Services Ltd
RAC House
PO Box 100
South Croydon CR2 6XW; tel. 081 686 2525
European Service tel. 081 686 0088

Useful words and phrases

Although English is often understood in the parts of Italy frequented by tourists, the visitor will undoubtedly find a few words and phrases of Italian very useful.

please	per favore
thank you (very much)	(molte) grazie
yes/no	si/no
excuse me	scusi (I beg your pardon), con permesso (when passing in front of someone)
do you speak English?	parla inglese?
I do not understand	non capisco
good morning	buon giorno
good evening	buona sera
goodbye	arrivederci
how much?	quanto?
I should like	vorrei avere
a room with a private bath	una camera con bagno
the bill, please (in restaurant)	cameriere, il conto!
everything included	tutto compreso
when?	quando?
open	aperto
shut	chiuso
where is .... street?	dov'è la via ...?
the road to ...?	la strada per ...?
how far is it to...?	quanto è distante ...?
to the left/right	a sinistra/a destra
straight on	sempre diritto
post office	ufficio postale
railway station	stazione
town hall	municipio
exchange office	ufficio di cambio
police station	posto di polizia
public telephone	telefono pubblico

tourist information office	ufficio turistico
doctor	medico
chemist's	farmacia
toilet	gabinetto
ladies	signore
gentlemen	signori
engaged	occupato
free	libero
entrance	entrata
exit	uscita
today/tomorrow	oggi/domani
Sunday/Monday	domenica/lunedì
Tuesday/Wednesday	martedì/mercoledì
Thursday/Friday	giovedì/venerdì
Saturday/holiday	sabato/giorno festivo

0	zero	8	otto
1	uno, una, un, un'	9	nove
2	due	10	dieci
3	tre	11	undici
4	quattro	12	dodici
5	cinque	20	venti
6	sei	50	cinquanta
7	sette	100	cento

Index

Agra 29
Alpino 35
Anfo 88
Angera 9, **30**, 31, 33
Arcumeggio 30
Argegno 48
Arona 30, **33f.**
Ascona 6, 40

Baveno 37
Belgirate 34
Bellagio 6, 52, **55**
Bellano 52
Bereguardo 82
Bergamo 4, 12, 18, 25, **76f.**
Birago di Camnago 11
Biumo Superiore 32
Bormio 4
Borromean islands 35ff.
Bossico 87
Brescia 12, 15, 18, 19, 76, **77f.**
Brianza 25
Brissago 40
Brunate 46

Ca del Ponte 10
Cadenabbia 5, 6, 9, 50, 52, 55
Camonica Valley 4, 18, 83
Campione 58f.
Campo dei Fiori 32f., 34
Cannero Riviera 39
Cannobio 39f.
Canzo 55
Capolago 59
Caprino 59
Carimate 11
Carmine Superiore 40
Cassina Rizzardi 11
Castagnola 59
Castiglione 48
Castro 87
Cerano 49
Cernobbio 47f.
Cerro 29
Cislano 86
Clusane 84
Colico 52
Colosso di San Carlone 33f.
Como 6, 9, 14, 18, 25, **46f.**
Como, Lake 3, 5, 9, 10, **44ff.**, 89
Corenno Plinio 52
Corgeno 31

Cremona 10, 19, 25, 76, **78f.**
Curtatone 13

Dumentina Valley 29
Dumenza 29

Fonteno 87
Fraine 86
Franciacorta 11, 23, 24, 83, 85

Garda, Lake 3, 9
Gignese 35
Goito 25
Gravedona 51
Griante 6, 50
Grigna 55

Idro 88
Idro, Lake 3, **87f.**
Intra 38
Iseo 84f.
Iseo, Lake 3, **83ff.**
Isola Bella 35, 36

Isola Comacina 44, 48
Isola Madre 35, 36f.
Isola dei Pescatori 35, 36
Isola di San Giulio 38
Ispra 30

Lago di Annone 54
Lago di Arengo 51
Lago di Comabbio 27, 31
Lago di Garlate 54
Lago di Mergozzo 3, 27, 38
Lago di Mezzola 51
Lago di Monate 27, 31
Lago di Olginate 54
Lago di Pusiano 54
Lago del Segrino 55
Lago di Varese 27, 31f.
Lainate 10
Laino 48
Laveno 29f., 30
Lecco 53f.
Legnano 13, 14
Lesa 34
Lezzeno 52

Basilica di Sant'Ambrogio, Milan

Index

Livigno 4
Locarno 6, 30, **40f.**, 42
Locarno Monti 41
Lovere 86f.
Lugano **57f.**, 59
Lugano, Lake 3, 9, **56ff.**
Luino 9, 25, **28f.**

Madesimo 4
Malenco Valley 11
Maggiore, Lake 3, 5, 6, 9, **27ff.**, 89
Magreglio 55
Mantua 4, 10, 15, 18, 76, **80f.**
Maroggia 59
Melide 59
Menaggio 11, 51, 52, 55
Milan 4f., 7, 11, 12, 13, 14, 15, 17, 18, 19, 21, 25, **61ff.**, 89, 91
  Basilica S. Lorenzo Maggiore 75
  Basilica di Sant' Ambrogio 74f.
  Brera (district) 65
  Castello Sforzesco 73f.
  Cimitero Monumentale 74
  Duomo 70f.
  Galleria Vittorio Emanuele 64, 71f.
  Museo Poldi Pezzoli 73
  Navigli 65
  Palazzo Reale 71

Milan (cont.)
  Pinacoteca di Brera 73
  Santa Maria delle Grazie 74
  Teatro alla Scala 72f.
Moltrasio 48
Monastero di Luvinate 11
Montagnola 58
Monte Isola 83, 86
Monte Mottarone 35, 37
Monte Rosso 38
Montorfano 11
Monza 11, 75

Oltrepò Pavese 4, 23, 82
Orta, Lake 3, 27, **37f.**
Orta San Giulio 37f.
Osteno 49

Pallanza 38
Parabiago 25
Paratico 84
Pavia 14, 15, 18, 19, **82**
Pella 38
Pigra 48
Pisogne 86
Po Valley 10, 14, 15, 17, 20, 23
Predore 87
Provaglio 85

Riva di Solto 87
Rodengo Saiano 85
Rovare Ispra 10
Rovato 85

Sacro Monte (Orta San Giulio) 38
Sacro Monte (Varese) 32f.
Sale Marasino 85
Santa Caterina del Sasso 30
Sarnico 87
Scaria 49
Stilfser pass 11
Stradella 25
Stresa 6, 34f.
Sulzano 85
S. Antonio 88
S. Fedele 49

Travedona-Monate 31
Tremezzo 6, 14, 50

Val d'Intelvi 48, 49
Val Sassina 52
Valtellina 4, 23, 24, 25, 52
Varenna 52f., 55
Varese 10, 19, 25, 32
Varesotto lakes 3, 31
Verbania 38f.
Verna 49
Verona 15
Vigevano 25, 82
Villa Carlotta 50
Villa La Collina 5, 50f.
Villa Taranto 38f.
Virginia (island) 32

Zone 86
Zorzino 87

Original German text: Sigmund Gottlieb. Translation: Wendy Bell
Series editor, English edition: Jane Rolph

© Verlag Robert Pfützner GmbH, München. Original German edition

© Jarrold Publishing, Norwich, Great Britain 1/91. English language edition worldwide

Published in the US and Canada by Hunter Publishing, Inc.,
300 Raritan Center Parkway, Edison NJ 08818

Illustrations: Claudia Bradlaw pages 47, 48; Douglas Dickins cover and pages 33, 41, 59; HSAG Limited pages 24, 60, 62, 66 (both), 67, 92; Italian State Tourist Board pages 4, 13, 29, 36, 53, 54, 58, 73, 75, 79, 81, 85, 95; Travel Trade Photography pages 1, 6, 19, 65, 72

The publishers have made every endeavour to ensure the accuracy of this publication but can accept no responsibility for any errors or omissions. They would, however, appreciate notification of any inaccuracies to correct future editions.

Printed in Italy

ISBN 0–7117–0476–7